Everglades National Park
Geologic Resource Evaluation Report

Natural Resource Report NPS/NRPC/GRD/NRR—2008/047

Geologic Resources Division
Natural Resource Program Center
P.O. Box 25287
Denver, Colorado 80225

September 2008

U.S. Department of the Interior
Washington, D.C.

The Natural Resource Publication series addresses natural resource topics that are of interest and applicability to a broad readership in the National Park Service and to others in the management of natural resources, including the scientific community, the public, and the NPS conservation and environmental constituencies. Manuscripts are peer-reviewed to ensure that the information is scientifically credible, technically accurate, appropriately written for the intended audience, and is designed and published in a professional manner.

Natural Resource Reports are the designated medium for disseminating high priority, current natural resource management information with managerial application. The series targets a general, diverse audience, and may contain NPS policy considerations or address sensitive issues of management applicability. Examples of the diverse array of reports published in this series include vital signs monitoring plans; "how to" resource management papers; proceedings of resource management workshops or conferences; annual reports of resource programs or divisions of the Natural Resource Program Center; resource action plans; fact sheets; and regularly-published newsletters.

Views, statements, findings, conclusions, recommendations and data in this report are solely those of the author(s) and do not necessarily reflect views and policies of the U.S. Department of the Interior, National Park Service. Mention of trade names or commercial products does not constitute endorsement or recommendation for use by the National Park Service.

Printed copies of reports in these series may be produced in a limited quantity and they are only available as long as the supply lasts. This report is also available online from the Geologic Resource Evaluation Program website (http://www2.nature.nps.gov/geology/inventory/gre_publications) and the Natural Resource Publication Management website (http://www.nature.nps.gov/publications/NRPM/index.cfm) or by sending a request to the address on the back cover.
Please cite this publication as:

Thornberry-Ehrlich, T. 2008. Everglades National Park Geologic Resource Evaluation Report. Natural Resource Report NPS/NRPC/GRD/NRR—2008/047. National Park Service, Denver, Colorado.

NPS D-345, September 2008

Table of Contents

List of Figures

Executive Summary

This report accompanies the digital geologic map for Everglades National Park in Florida, which the Geologic Resources Division produced in collaboration with its partners. It contains information relevant to resource management and scientific research.

The environment of south Florida including the Everglades is among the most unique on earth. Habitats at Everglades National Park include open marine areas, estuaries, mangrove zones, buttonwood ridges, coastal prairies, freshwater sloughs, freshwater marl prairies, cypress groves, tree islands, hardwood hammocks, and pinelands. Geology has a profound influence on these environments. It affects surface water flow and contributes to climate, hydrology, and topography in Florida. Geologic units and structures provide the foundation for the development of all ecosystems.

With its low-lying topography, south Florida has been alternately submerged and exposed with variations in sea level for the past 50,000 years. The Everglades area is one of the lowest, youngest, and most geologically stable platforms of North America. This overall stability belies incredibly dynamic geologic processes at work on the landscape of south Florida. Beneath the surface at Everglades National Park, there are thousands of meters of roughly horizontal geologic units rich in carbonate minerals. These minerals dissolve in acidic solution. Rainwater and groundwater rich in decaying organic materials have dissolved interconnected void networks in the subsurface of south Florida. This dissolution ultimately results in a karst landscape characterized by solution holes, sinkholes, disappearing streams, springs, and incredible water storage capacity.

The storage capacity of the rocks underlying Everglades National Park is the reason the unique ecosystems have flourished there through inhospitable drought seasons,

fire danger, and seasonal hurricanes. Aquifers at various stratigraphic levels including the Biscayne unconfined surficial aquifer support the habitats at Everglades. These vast water resources attracted human populations to the area as well.

From the late 1800s, human development has steadily increased in south Florida. Drastic measures were taken to drain swamps for agriculture and urban development. Canals, ditches, dams, and levees forever altered the once steady, slow flow of fresh water from Lake Okeechobee south to Florida Bay along the "River of Grass" – the Everglades. An intense, multiagency cooperative research effort is underway to restore the Everglades and preserve what remains of the once vast wetland environment of South Florida. An increased understanding of geologic resources must play a key role in these efforts at Everglades National Park.

The following selected geologic issues (listed in detail with others identified by GRE scoping meeting participants, plus suggestions for inventory, monitoring, and research in the *Geologic Issues* section) have geological importance and a high level of resource management significance within the park:

- Anthropogenic Impacts,
- Aquifer Characteristics and Groundwater Flow Dynamics,
- Storm-influenced Sediment Transport Dynamics, and
- Near Coastal Response to Sea Level Rise.

Introduction

The following section briefly describes the National Park Service Geologic Resource Evaluation Program and the regional geologic setting of Everglades National Park.

Purpose of the Geologic Resource Evaluation Program

The Geologic Resource Evaluation (GRE) Program is one of 12 inventories funded under the NPS Natural Resource Challenge designed to enhance baseline information available to park managers. The program carries out the geologic component of the inventory effort from the development of digital geologic maps to providing park staff with a geologic report tailored to a park's specific geologic resource issues. The Geologic Resources Division of the Natural Resource Program Center administers this program. The GRE team relies heavily on partnerships with the U.S. Geological Survey, Colorado State University, state surveys, and others in developing GRE products.

The goal of the GRE Program is to increase understanding of the geologic processes at work in parks and provide sound geologic information for use in park decision making. Sound park stewardship relies on understanding natural resources and their role in the ecosystem. Geology is the foundation of park ecosystems. The compilation and use of natural resource information by park managers is called for in section 204 of the National Parks Omnibus Management Act of 1998 and in NPS-75, Natural Resources Inventory and Monitoring Guideline.

To realize this goal, the GRE team is systematically working towards providing each of the identified 270 natural area parks with a geologic scoping meeting, a digital geologic map, and a geologic report. These products support the stewardship of park resources and are designed for non-geoscientists. During scoping meetings the GRE team brings together park staff and geologic experts to review available geologic maps and discuss specific geologic issues, features, and processes.

The GRE mapping team converts the geologic maps identified for park use at the scoping meeting into digital geologic data in accordance with their innovative Geographic Information Systems (GIS) Data Model. These digital data sets bring an exciting interactive dimension to traditional paper maps by providing geologic data for use in park GIS and facilitating the incorporation of geologic considerations into a wide range of resource management applications. The newest maps come complete with interactive help files. As a companion to the digital geologic maps, the GRE team prepares a park-specific geologic report that aids in use of the maps and provides park managers with an overview of park geology and geologic resource management issues.

For additional information regarding the content of this report and up to date GRE contact information please refer to the Geologic Resource Evaluation Web site (http://www.nature.nps.gov/geology/inventory/).

Geologic Setting

Everglades National Park protects over 1,508,537 acres (fig. 1). The park contains some of the most pristine and unique marshland habitat in the continental United States and is the only subtropical preserve in North America. Everglades National Park was established under Harry S. Truman's administration on December 6, 1947. On October 26, 1976, the park became an International Biosphere Reserve and it attained Wilderness Designation on November 10, 1978. The park was made a world heritage site on October 24, 1979, and named a Wetland of International Importance on June 4, 1987.

This vast park spans the southern tip of the Florida peninsula and most of Florida Bay between the peninsula and the Florida Keys. The environments at the park vary from mangrove and cypress swamps, marine and estuarine environments, pinelands and hardwood hammocks, to sawgrass prairies and rock ridges. The area covers a large portion of the Florida Bay, a large carbonate mud bank.

South Florida lies within the Atlantic Coastal Plain physiographic province, one of 5 major physiographic provinces in the eastern United States (fig. 2). In the area of the Everglades, it is divided into several physiographic subprovinces – Everglades, Atlantic Coastal Ridge, Big Cypress Swamp, and Sandy Flatlands. The Everglades subprovince forms a south dipping, spoon-shaped low-lying area between the Atlantic Coastal Ridge to the east, the Big Cypress Swamp to the west, and the Sandy Flatlands area to the north. The basin has very low relief. The elevation change is only 3.6–4.3 m (12–14 ft) from the maximum near Lake Okeechobee to sea level at Florida Bay. Prior to anthropogenic alteration in the form of canals, ditches, and dams, this drainage system flowed slowly and steadily from north to south.

Bounding the Everglades province on the east is the Atlantic Coastal Ridge subprovince. It is comprised of Pleistocene marine limestones covered by thin quartz sand sheets. The marine limestone is composed of tiny ooids of carbonate that were pushed into a linear ridge by long shore currents during the Pleistocene Epoch (1.8 Ma to 10,000 years ago). The province ranges in elevation from 1.5–6 m (5–20 ft) in the southernmost portions. The width of the ridge ranges from 16 km (10 mi) in southern Miami-Dade County and narrows to 5–8 km (3–5 mi) further north. Periodically breaching the southern portions of the ridge are sloughs (transverse marshes) oriented perpendicular to the trend of the ridge.

The southern reaches of the Everglades and Big Cypress Swamp subprovinces transition into the Coastal Marshes and Mangrove Swamp subsection. The subsection covers an area from the northeastern part of Florida Bay, around the southern Florida peninsula, and west, into the Gulf of Mexico up to the Ten Thousand Island region near Everglades City. Bands of swamps and brackish marshes sitting just above sea level characterize this subprovince. Freshwater runoff and tidal fluxes cause the salinity to change dramatically. This is why the mangrove, capable of enduring such salinity changes, thrives in this area.

The Big Cypress Swamp subprovince defines the western boundary of the Everglades. The rocks underlying this area are among the oldest in South Florida composed of silts, sands, and carbonates. This area is slightly higher in elevation than the Everglades basin because it is underlain primarily by the coral-rich limestones of the Pliocene Tamiami Formation (3–4 Ma). This formation is exposed in large areas of Big Cypress National Preserve and in the northwest corner of Everglades National Park. Drainage in the subprovince is primarily to the south and southwest.

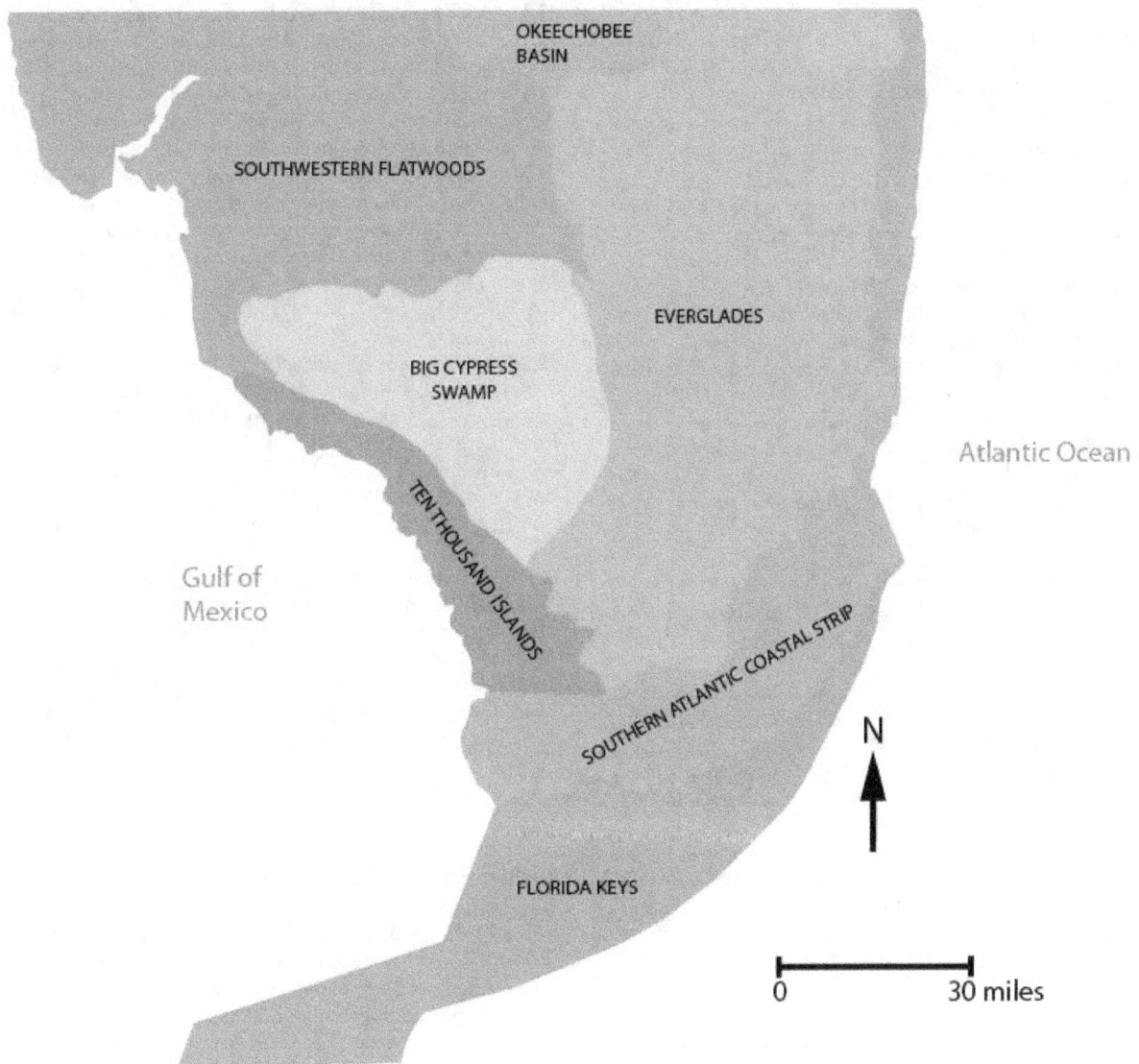

Figure 2: Map of physiographic subsections in South Florida as defined by Brooks (1981). This map delineates subsections of larger physiographic subprovinces in South Florida. The Southern Atlantic Coastal Strip roughly corresponds to the Atlantic Coastal Ridge subprovince in the eastern areas and in southern reaches along with the Ten Thousand Islands area it corresponds to the Coastal Marshes and Mangroves subprovince described in the text. The Devils Garden and areas north correspond approximately to the Sandy Flatlands subprovince. Data provided by St. Johns River Water Management District www.sjrwmd.com (accessed February 21, 2006). Graphic is by Trista L. Thornberry-Ehrlich (Colorado State University). .

Geologic Issues

A Geologic Resource Evaluation scoping session was held for Everglades National Park on January 24–25, 2005, to discuss geologic resources, address the status of geologic mapping, and assess resource management issues and needs. This section synthesizes the scoping results, in particular those issues that may require attention from resource managers.

This section discusses the management of natural resources and lists the most critical topics first. Potential research projects and other topics of scientific interest are presented at the end of this section.

Anthropogenic Impacts

Since the late 1800s, humans have been the single most significant force of landscape change in the Everglades. Drainage of the vast wetlands was once considered necessary for safety, commerce, and inhabitation. The gently flowing water of south Florida was manipulated into 1,600 km (1,000 mi) of canals and 1,200 km (720 mi) of levees as part of the Central and South Florida Project authorized by Congress in 1948 (fig. 3). Overall flow is now controlled by 16 pump stations and over 200 gates and other structures. Approximately half of the Everglades' "River of Grass" has been developed for agricultural and urban use. Rivers and sloughs, such as, the Kissimmee River have been destroyed or converted to canal systems (FDEP 2005).

A comprehensive study of the impacts of water flow manipulation is beyond the scope of this report; however, a short summary appears below. For more information, the Water Resource Division of the National Park Service has prepared a baseline inventory of water quality data for Everglades National Park which is available online (http://nrdata.nps.gov/EVER/nrdata/water/baseline_wq/docs/EVERWQAA.pdf, Accessed July 15, 2008). Numerous interagency, cooperative programs such as the Everglades Program, the Everglades Construction Project, the Everglades Forever Act, and CERP are vital to the restoration and ecosystem health of the Everglades. Everglades National Park needs to continue to support and engage in efforts that affect the entire south Florida ecosystem.

The results of anthropogenic water flow manipulation to the environment are dramatic and not well understood. The complex ecosystem is now largely engineered and is no longer buffered by the long-term water storage once inherent to south Florida. An average of 1.7 billion gallons of water discharges daily to the ocean and water flow to the Everglades has declined by approximately 70%. Low freshwater input to Florida Bay is causing hypersaline conditions, seagrass decline, fish depopulation, and algal blooms. Low water levels (drought) cause fire danger whereas flooding threatens tree island and hardwood hammock ecosystems. Estimates are that 90–95% of the wading bird population has been lost and 68 plant and animal species are threatened or endangered in south Florida (FDEP 2005).

Hydraulic gradients in Florida naturally push water from north to south causing dissolved toxins to accumulate in south Florida. Lake Okeechobee is eutrophied meaning it is so rich in mineral and organic nutrients that a proliferation of plant life, especially algae is reducing the overall dissolved oxygen content causing harm to other organisms. This lack of oxygen combined with increases in dissolved toxins pose serious threats to the aquatic ecosystems in the Everglades. In addition, many thousands of acres of Everglades marsh have been invaded by cattails and other opportunistic species (FDEP 2005).

In 2007, Everglades National Park hosted 1,074,764 visitors, placing increasing demands on the limited resources and fragile ecosystem of the park. Motorized boat access and fishing are restricted in the wilderness areas of the park. Concerns range from overuse of backcountry facilities, waste and pollution, and effects on the hydrologic system at the park due to visitor use.

Water quality is a constant problem at Everglades National Park. Problems range from reductions in dissolved oxygen, pH, alkalinity and salinity changes, to high levels of pollutants such as nitrate, phosphorous, bacteria, mercury, and pesticides (SFWMD 2002). Mercury contamination of the surface water is affecting fish and bird of prey populations. There is a need to quantitatively study the interaction between groundwater flow and the overall fresh water and marine ecological quality in the Everglades.

Earthen and Failed Dams, Canals, and Sheet Piling

Dams and other earth works in the park pose a serious threat to the safety of visitors and park resources. During the 1930's, a series of canals and levees were constructed (including East Cape canal, Homestead canal, Slegel's ditch, Houseman's ditch, and Middle Cape canal) to divert the water away from the "prime" real estate around Cape Sable. The real estate venture failed and the land was later included in the Everglades National Park boundaries. The remediation and management of the canals and earth works is a park responsibility.

Canals, dams, and ditches throughout south Florida divert water away from the natural flow between Lake Okeechobee and the Everglades. Locally, near Cape Sable and Lake Ingraham, the flow is disrupted and sediment transport patterns have changed. Fresh water marshes behind the cape are being salinated due to the overall lack of fresh water input.

In 2005, as a response to a technical assistance request, hydrologists and geomorphologists from the Water Resources Division, Geologic Resources Division, and Southeast Region of the NPS prepared a report evaluating the restoration alternatives for the Cape Sable area canals at Everglades National Park. These canals have caused visitor safety problems and substantially affected coastal morphology, sediment transport and deposition, and fresh–salt water exchange dynamics. Alternatives ranged from no action to active remediation such as concrete structures and plugs (Crisfield et al., 2005). The report, available from the Geologic Resources Division, includes detailed descriptions of the area, the history of human modifications there, and remediation suggestions.

Aquifer Characteristics and Groundwater Flow Dynamics

The karst aquifer system of south Florida is open to numerous inputs of water from precipitation, surface flow, and artificial diversions (canals, ditches, ponds, etc.). The underlying Miami Limestone and Fort Thompson Formation form the Biscayne aquifer in the upper part of the surficial aquifer beneath Everglades National Park. The Fort Thompson Formation, underlying the Miami Limestone, is riddled with well-developed solution cavities and conduit networks rendering it highly permeable. The Miami Limestone is less permeable, lacking the same degree of connectivity between cavities (Bruno et al. 2003).

Understanding the nature of the hydrologic exchange between surface and ground waters is critical to understanding the movement of water and dissolved nutrients, wastes, metals, etc. in the Everglades ecosystem (Bruno et al. 2003). Knowledge of this exchange has direct ties to understanding the hydrogeologic system of the unconfined Biscayne aquifer beneath the park.

Inventory, Monitoring, and Research Suggestions for Aquifer Characteristics and Groundwater Flow Dynamics

- Determine how many wells are necessary to model the hydrogeologic system at the park.
- Model the porosity and permeability of the Fort Thompson Formation.
- Continue studies using ground-penetrating radar, borehole data, and cores for characterization of the aquifers beneath the park (Cunningham 2004a). These techniques can also identify karstic characteristics of the subsurface.
- Examine the salt wedge characteristics versus the surface water.
- Determine if a change in hydraulic head at the Everglades would create positive or negative impacts on the overall ecosystem health.
- Identify the extent of near-surface voids at Everglades National Park.
- Survey and map fine-scale topographic variations at the park to apply to hydrogeologic models. Use this

information to determine the nature of the divide between Taylor and Shark River Sloughs.
- Continue studies of copepod species composition and distribution in the subsurface habitats at Everglades to better understand the exchange between surface and ground water (Bruno et al. 2003).

Storm-influenced Sediment Transport Dynamics

Because Florida sits as a peninsular boundary between the Gulf of Mexico and the Atlantic Ocean, it exerts a significant influence on climate. The peninsula marks the climatic zone boundary between semi-tropical and temperate zones. Convective heating around the Florida peninsula is pronounced during the summer months causing the development of large cumulonimbus storm systems and thunderstorms (Holmes and Miller 2004). Hurricanes are common between the months of May and October in the Caribbean Sea. These storms and seasonal hurricanes, influenced by Florida's geologic setting, send torrents of rain to south Florida and are a vital component of the Everglades ecosystem with a pronounced effect on the landscape. Storm events have the potential to damage facilities and release toxins trapped in deep sediments and muds. With high-energy erosive events followed by flooding, these pollutants may be redistributed within the ecosystem.

Determining baseline conditions would benefit resource management in predicting and understanding the environmental response to storm events. Hurricane Donna in 1960 evacuated water from Florida Bay by about 1 m (3 ft), before the water rushed back in to a depth of 2.1 m (7 ft). This resulted in mud deposition on the south side of the mud ridges and a high-energy shell layer deposit on the north side. In 1992, Hurricane Andrew caused extreme erosion that completely removed the highland beach area near the Ross River. Geochemical changes resulting from the influx of storm water went unmeasured during cleanup and restoration operations by local agencies. In 2005, many park facilities were damaged by hurricanes Katrina and Wilma at Everglades National Park. The Flamingo area suffered storm surges and flooding. Marinas and other areas were filled with mud and storm debris. These events also affected the natural environment at Everglades National Park.

The very nature of the landscape at the Everglades is one of relatively rapid change. Shifting muds and sands continually alter the shape and profile of the shoreline. Sand and mud erode from one beach and are deposited elsewhere in the course of a single storm event. Understanding the sediment transport dynamics at the park, especially within Florida Bay and the coastal areas such as Cape Sable, would provide important information to park resource managers.

Cape Sable is located along the southwestern coast of Everglades National Park. It contains a variety of features including Lake Ingraham, Bear Lake, Little Fox, Middle Fox, and East Fox Lakes, Coot Bay, Mud Bay, and many wave swept beach areas such as Northwest Cape, Middle Cape, East Cape, and Clubhouse Beach. It also contains remnants of manufactured canals, levees, and ditches created in an attempt to render the area viable real estate during the 1930s. Cape Sable is host to numerous rare species including the Cape Sable seaside sparrow, diamondback terrapin (*Malaclemys terrapin*), loggerhead (*Caretta caretta*), Indopacific gecko (*Hemidactylus garnotii*), and eastern hog nose snake (*Heterodon platyrhinos*). Cape Sable is separated from the mainland by Whitewater Bay. This brackish environment is fed by the Shark, Broad, and Harney Rivers and is bounded by a buttonwood embankment growing as a natural berm on a mud storm beach.

The hydrogeologic system in the area around Lake Ingraham was altered with the construction of canals, roads, and levees. As a result, sediments scouring through the canals are being deposited in the lake basin (6–30 cm/year [2.4–11.8 in/year]). Lake levels are very low and the lake basin sediments are often exposed at low tide. The delta emanating from the Middle Cape Canal is expanding and increasing the sediment influx for the Florida Bay. Salinity is increasing as 80 high tides a year crest the low marl ridges. This erodes the ridges, transporting their material into the basins behind them. With local sea level rise, higher salinity waters are encroaching on the fresh water areas. This leads to a decline in marsh, mangrove, and prairie areas.

Inventory, Monitoring, and Research Suggestions for Storm-influenced Sediment Transport Dynamics

- Use sediment transport models and vegetation maps in a GIS to study declines in mangrove, marsh, and prairie areas. This decline may be related to the canal system or due to sea level rise around Lake Ingraham, or both. Sediment transport models may also be useful in determining if artificial structures should be destroyed or reestablished based on predicted ecosystem response.

- Identify potential remediation efforts for eroded canal openings (erosion rate is 0.6–1.2 m/year, [2–4 ft/year]).

- Determine the nature of the relationship between the diversion of water through canals and the buttonwood ridge distribution.

- Develop a response protocol in cooperation with other local agencies to determine the geochemical effects of storm surges.

- Perform a local inventory of selected sites to determine the recovery rates of mangrove zones and buttonwood ridges after large storm events.

- Establish baselines of topography, mud composition and distribution, etc. for comparison and prediction of response to future events.

Near Coastal Response to Sea Level Rise

Sea level rise is affecting all of South Florida. While slowing the rate of sea level rise is beyond the resources of the park, monitoring sea level change, evaluating, and predicting impacts on the park's landscape and ecosystem is an important management issue. Topography is among the controlling factors in ecosystem development at Everglades National Park. Topographic variations in part define the extent of habitats such as marine-estuary, coastal prairie,

mangrove zones, sloughs, marl prairies, hammocks, pinelands, and cypress swamps. The scale of inches is important for the low banks and ridges where the tides and wind expose the entire western basins.

Because of the low elevation and small topographic relief, a small change in sea level has the ability to affect millions of acres of Everglades. Already, saline water is inundating low-lying areas, especially during storm events. The fresh water marshes and brackish estuaries are under constant threat of inundation by the sea. Given the low relief of the park, continued rise will destroy much of the marsh landscape protected at the park including the mangrove zones, mud ridges and other coastal features, which normally buffer the freshwater wetlands from marine inundation.

Mangrove zones and buttonwood ridges skirt the southern Florida coast where oscillating fresh and saline water conditions dominate. Here red (*Rhizophora mangle*), black (*Avicennia germinans*), and white mangroves (*Laguncularia racemosa*) thrive. In a sense, these zones define the water level and anchor shorelines. They form a buffering zone between the open waters of the coast and the freshwater uplands and wetlands. They also provide a nursery for shrimp and fish, and vital nutrients as well as shelter and nesting areas for open-water predators and several species of birds (SFWMD 2002). A baseline needs to be established regarding sea level rise to determine its effect on the mangrove areas. Detailed topographic data would help manage this resource.

In Florida Bay, sea level rise is 23 cm (9 in) in 70 years of recorded measurements. The Florida Bay is covered by an extensive system of supra- and subtidal carbonate mud banks, seagrass beds, coastal marl ridges, coastal carbonate mud ridges, mangrove peat deposits, and mollusk deposits. The bay stretches from the southern coast of Florida to the Florida Keys island reef tract over an area of 2,850 km^2 (1,100 mi^2) (NOAA 2006). This environment is incredibly dynamic and unique. The features in the bay are strongly related to minute changes in elevation. Environments within the bay can change within centimeters of topographic relief. Understanding the movement of water around Florida Bay and what buttressing effect, if any, the mud and marl ridges have on water flow patterns is essential for resource management. Many of the freshwater marshes behind the ridges are changing to super saline marine lagoons because of sea level rise.

Given the topographic control on the distribution of the various environments in Florida Bay and the coverage of mapping at the park, normal surficial maps are not sufficient for complex management decisions at the Everglades. An interdisciplinary approach to mapping is critical to producing a useful product for resource management. Anthropogenic, supratidal, intertidal, subtidal, and coastal features would all be helpful. This holistic ecosystem approach integrates biological, physical, cultural, and oceanographic parameters. Lidar surveys in addition to satellite imagery, multibeam mapping, bathymetry data, water quality and circulation, shoreline change data, pre- and post-storm comparisons, oceanographic data (waves, tides, currents, turbidity, temperature salinity, sediment transport patterns, coral larvae and other species distributions), etc. are essential for resource management at Everglades National Park.

Sea level rise is also causing beach erosion near Cape Sable and Lake Ingraham. Increases in turbidity and changing currents with rising seas are causing large seagrass dieoffs and increased carbonate material suspension.

Inventory, Monitoring, and Research Suggestions for Near Coastal Response to Sea Level Rise

- Quantitatively correlate the relationship between coastal marl and carbonate mud ridges and the buttonwood distribution using new mapping and GIS.

- Determine the minimum mapping unit for Florida Bay relevant to resource management.

- Using new topographic mapping and current data, determine the flow dynamics (especially related to salinity patterns) in the bay.

- Research potential remediation procedures for the hypersaline environments in the central portion of Florida Bay.

- Research potential methods to protect the subaerial habitat in the coastal areas from rising sea level.

- Continue monitoring the local rate of sea level rise.

- Using storm surge data and information, model buttonwood and mangrove zone response to rising seas.

- Monitor and measure the relationship between water level flux and elevations to determine an exposure/submergence index (i.e. 100% of the time exposed versus 0% of the time exposed).

- Establish the height of buttonwood ridges and correlate this spatially with their distribution.

- Identify the minimum mapping unit for buttonwood ridge and mangrove zone topographic mapping.

- Perform fine-scale topographic mapping of the southern coastal areas to monitor and predict ecosystem response to fluctuating water levels and freshwater vs. saline water input.

Atmospheric Deposition of African Dust

Fine dust has been blowing across the Atlantic Ocean and deposited in south Florida for thousands of years. The dust is an aggregate of clay and quartz particles cemented with iron oxides (Holmes and Miller 2004). This dust is derived from the deserts, dry lake and streambeds, and plains of Africa. Paleosols and reddish (oxidized) layers atop the Miami Limestone attest to these airborne inputs (fig. 4). The process continues today, but human occupation and modern development on the African continent has introduced nutrients, elements, microbes, pesticides, soot, organics, bacteria, viruses, and other contaminants to the dust.

Microbes and bacteria in the dust could pose biological threats to plant and animal species, not to mention

humans. The fine dust diminishes air and water visibility. A peak of dust fall in the 1980s coincided with a sea urchin disease and other benthic die-offs in south Florida. Lead, arsenic, phosphate, copper, iron, and mercury concentrations in the surface sediments in the middle of Florida Bay are highest in low tidal flux areas. Toxic concentrations may be liberated to exposure during high tide, hurricane, and other storm surge events. Mercury, arsenic and other metals are significantly higher in samples collected throughout south Florida than average crustal rocks. African dust supplies close to 25% of the arsenic deposited in soils in the southeastern United States (Holmes and Miller 2004). Awareness of this potential issue may help resource management anticipate environmental response to the contaminants in airborne dust.

Inventory, Monitoring, and Research Suggestions for Atmospheric Deposition of African Dust

- Expand and utilize the many 9.1 m (30 ft) monitoring wells in Florida Bay to identify and measure contaminant concentrations in dust, monitor rate of dust deposition, etc. (Gene Shinn, personal communication 2005).

- Spatially monitor dust levels and study potential correlations with environmental responses such as hypersalinity and dieoffs.

Miscellaneous Issues and General Geologic Research Potential

Major ongoing research and restoration efforts

Everglades National Park has been the site of intense scientific interest and ecosystem restoration efforts for decades. Multiple research studies are ongoing. A wealth of information exists on the ecosystem at the park and a major multi-agency effort is underway with the goals of understanding the controls on this ecosystem, determining the best ways to restore it, and finding ways for humans to coexist with the natural Everglades. Agencies such as the National Park Service, the U.S. Geological Survey, the National Oceanic and Atmospheric Administration, the U.S. Army Corps of Engineers, the Florida Geological Survey, and the South Florida Water Management District among many others are making strides to accomplish these goals.

Useful resources for up-to-date information on research and restoration efforts for Everglades National Park include the South Florida Water Management District's Living Everglades website (http://glades.sfwmd.gov/empact/home/index.shtml), the website for the Comprehensive Everglades Restoration Plan (CERP) (http://fl.water.usgs.gov/CERP/cerp.html), and the U.S. Geological Survey's South Florida Information Access (SOFIA) integrated science website (http://sofia.usgs.gov/).

Paleoclimates

Cores from Florida and Biscayne Bays, and numerous sloughs in the park contain peat and pollen which can serve as representative indicators of past climates.

Pleistocene and Holocene climatic shifts are relevant to establish baseline data for future predictions and to interpret modern patterns. Increasing the spatial density of cores would improve efforts to determine the temporal relationships of climate shifts and to make accurate interpolations between points for recreating past landscapes.

Bioturbation, agriculture, quarrying, and other ground disturbances (e.g., railroad infill effects) distort the subsurface features. More unconsolidated sediment core studies would increase coverage and understanding of paleoclimates at the Everglades. Further identification of pollen species is vital to this goal.

Archaeological Sites

There are several sites, approximately 12,000 years old, along ancient coastlines and within hardwood hammocks and tree islands that contain artifacts from local indigenous populations. Artifacts include pottery fragments, tools made of material obtained through trading with northern indigenous groups, and other implements. Mapping and/or reconstructing these sites

would add to the cultural value of the park. An interesting interpretive story may describe how people lived in this wetland environment before roads, trails and other facilities were in place. These studies may additionally help reconstruct the location and pattern of change of the paleoshoreline in the Ten Thousand Lakes, and Cape Sable areas.

"Lake Belt" Management

The term "Lake Belt" refers to a series of quarries near the park. These features are intended to supply water to the park as part of a restoration effort. There is some concern about how these features are affecting groundwater movement. Some USGS monitoring wells are located near levees, but more wells would increase understanding of the local hydrogeologic system.

Local agriculture introduces sulphates, phosphorus, and other contaminants into the groundwater near these lakes that, given the permeable, conduit-rich bedrock, could easily contaminate the water in the quarries and affect the ecosystem of the park.

Figure 3: Trench dug through surficial geologic units near Rock Reef Pass at Everglades National Park. Photograph is by Trista L. Thornberry-Ehrlich (Colorado State University).

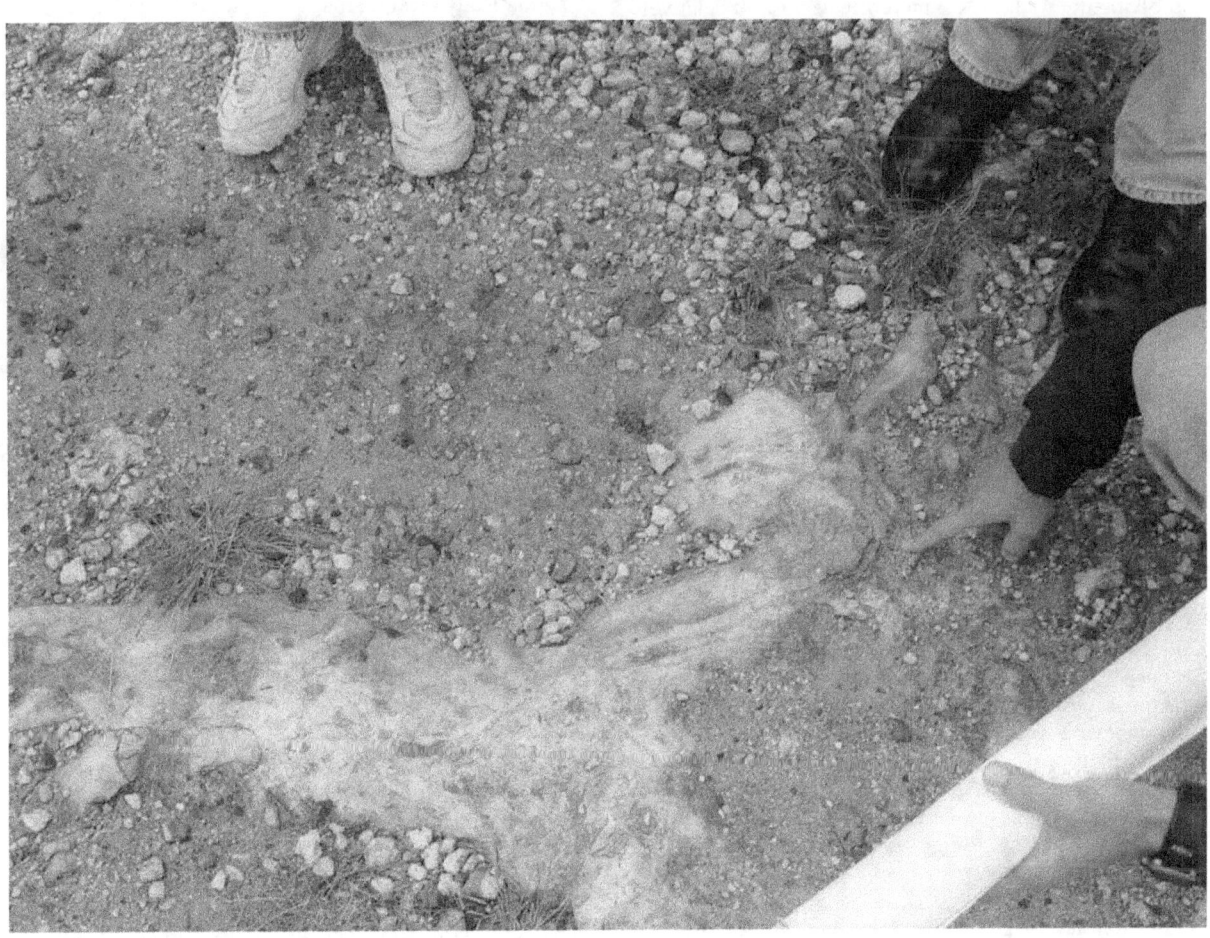

Figure 4: Reddish layer of African dust deposition in bedrock at Elliot Key of nearby Biscayne National Park. Photograph by Trista L. Thornberry-Ehrlich (Colorado State University).

Geologic Features and Processes

This section describes the most prominent and distinctive geologic features and processes in Everglades National Park.

Karst Landscape

Karstic landforms are nearly synonymous with south Florida. Karst is a term that refers to a characteristic terrain produced by the chemical erosion of limestone or dolomite (carbonate rocks). Dissolution occurs when acidic meteoric water and groundwater undersaturated with respect to calcium carbonate react with carbonate rock surfaces along cracks and fractures slowly dissolving the rocks. Most meteoric water is of relatively low pH in the form of acid rain and becomes more acidic as it flows through decaying plant debris and soils (FGS 2005). Most of the limestones and dolomites in the Everglades are inherently porous.

At Everglades National Park, the dominant surficial geologic units include the Miami Limestone and the underlying shallow water limestone of the Fort Thompson Formation. These units comprise the uppermost 17 m of cored section in the Everglades. The Miami Limestone is ~125 – 130 thousand years old and contains two facies, the oolitic facies and the bryozoan facies, which intermingle in most of the outcrops at Everglades National Park (Cunningham 2005). These carbonate units are susceptible to dissolution.

Over hundreds of thousands of years since the last significant interglacial period led to the flooding of the Florida platform (approximately 130 thousand years ago), dissolution has occurred between the intergranular pores and along fractures altering the rock and creating larger and larger voids (fig. 5). The system of underground voids and conduits in south Florida is extensive. Collapse of overlying rock and soil into a void produces a solution hole (also referred to as a sinkhole), which may be connected to an underground conduit (fig. 6). If the solution hole occurs in a streambed, it may capture the water flow creating a disappearing stream. When groundwater, under hydraulic pressure, discharges from an underground drainage system, a spring is formed (FGS 2005).

Solution holes are an obvious element of the karst topography at the park. Large solution holes formed in the Miami Limestone when sea level and the water table were lower than present levels. As sea level has increased during the Holocene (a trend that continues in south Florida), many of the lower elevation solution holes have filled with organic material and marl. As organic material continues to decay, lowering the pH of the groundwater with inputs of carbonic acid, further dissolution of the near surface limestones continues at Everglades National Park. Many of the larger solution holes found in the pinelands are likely due to the collapse of small subsurface caves (fig. 6) (Cunningham 2005). Open cavities or threat of future collapse may compromise visitor safety; however, they are a vital component to the ecosystem providing essential habitat for fish and other wildlife especially during the dry winter months at Everglades National Park. Solution holes often fill with peat and other organic material that support larger tree species. If build up of peat continues, in time, a tree island or hardwood hammock may develop.

Solution holes (approximately 50) occur throughout the park (especially in the eastern half) and need to be systematically located, mapped, and described in terms of distribution, depth, interconnectedness, and other characteristics for resource management decision making. It is unknown how these solution holes impact the hydrogeologic regime including retention time, hydraulic head, and water storage. Potential data sources include aerial photography and field surveys. Continued research would be necessary to determine the degree of active dissolution, and the connectivity between subsurface conduits.

Borrow pits and canals intersect the permeable geologic units in many locations of the park, affecting local water flow (fig. 3). A hydrogeologic model detailing how water flows in the park with respect to karst features and artificial features such as canals and ditches would be a valuable resource management tool.

Florida Bay

Simply defined, Florida Bay is a shallow inner-shelf lagoon located between the mainland and the Florida Keys island reef tract. It is the southern terminus of the south Florida watershed. However, Florida Bay is anything but simple. Freshwater, flowing from the Everglades, mixes with salt water from the Gulf of Mexico in this shallow basin forming a vast estuary. The bay is approximately 2,850 km^2 (1,100 mi^2) of mangrove islands and peat deposits, interconnected basins, grassy supra- and subtidal carbonate mud banks, mud-mounds, coastal marl and carbonate mud ridges, and open shallow water. The average water depth of the bay is only 1 m (3 ft); thus the features in the bay and the corresponding ecosystem are strongly related to minute changes in elevation on the order of centimeters of relief (FLMNH 2006; NOAA 2006)

A bottom type survey of Florida Bay was conducted by the U.S. Geological Survey in 1996–1997. The bottom types surveyed did not include mangrove islands. Bottom types were primarily defined on the basis of seagrass density and sediment texture as well as overall structure. Bottom types included bank top suite, open mud, hardbottom, sparse seagrass cover, intermediate seagrass cover, dense seagrass cover, mixed bottom suite, and open sandy areas (fig. 7) (Prager and Halley 1997). Bank top suite refers to bottom types including mud banks at depths typically less than 0.6 m (2 ft) dominated by carbonate mud, sand, and locally, gravel in a series of linear sedimentary facies (Bosence 1995; Prager and

Halley 1997). Open mud is used to describe areas where little to no seagrass cover (or other benthic fauna except algal mats) is present. These may be areas of former seagrass dieoff (Prager and Halley 1997).

Hardbottom is the term used to describe areas with little to no benthic fauna cover as in open mud; however, unconsolidated sediment thickness in hardbottom is 5 cm (2 in) or less. Sparse to dense seagrass cover refers to areas in which 50 to 100% of the bottom is exposed. *Penincilus, Batophora,* and scattered sponges occur in these areas. Sediments are muddy carbonate sands, sandy mud, or sand and are often up to 2 m (6 ft) thick. Seagrass tends to trap sediments in these areas. Mixed bottom suite as the name suggests, describes highly variable bottom areas. Variations in sea grass density, open mud areas, and sediment type are spatially extreme. Open sandy areas generally occur in the boundary areas between the Gulf of Mexico and Florida Bay. No significant life is present in these areas of coarse shelly carbonate sands (Prager and Halley 1997).

Much study has been devoted to understanding the origin and anatomy of biodetrital mud-mounds. Early study suggested these features were biogenic structures formed by trapping and binding of algal aragonitic mud. Later research indicated the mud was both calcite and aragonite derived from the in situ breakdown of shell material in the bay. Current studies indicate these mounds initiate as aggradational grass-bed deposits and packstones, which are overlain with layered mudstones and erosional (winnowed) surfaces. Wind-driven (storm) currents flow from the northeast to the southwest scouring winnowed grainstones and mud-pebble conglomerates from the mounds to deposit on the leeward side. Currents from the southeast represent fair-weather flow. Thus, the morphology and distribution of the mounds and other depositional features in Florida Bay are a complex response to storm influenced physical erosion and redeposition of sediments and fair-weather biogenic and physical deposition processes (Bosence 1995).

South Florida has predominantly been a site of carbonate accumulation since the Mesozoic Era. These sediments are thousands of meters thick. Beneath the Florida Bay lime muds accumulated and slowly turned to rock forming Pleistocene-age limestones. Much of this mud is biogenic and forms slowly. Other deposits within Florida bay come from the breaking down of shell material and storm driven deposition (Shinn et al. 1997).

Understanding landscape evolution during late Holocene sea level rise (a 23 cm [9 in] rise in sea level in 70 years) may prove critical to predicting future response to sea level changes. Because Florida Bay is such a broad, shallow basin, even moderate sea level rise is expected to have significant impacts to the biota and environments found there. This response is poorly understood and change is occurring at alarming rates. Many of the freshwater marshes behind the mud ridges are changing to super saline marine lagoons as less freshwater (50% reduction over the past century) infiltrates the bay from the northern watershed (FLNHM 2006). As sea level

rises, many of the low-lying mangrove forest areas may be flooded. Florida Bay has experienced seagrass die-offs, algal blooms, and declining populations in indigenous sponges, shellfish, and other species (Brewster-Wingard 2001). How these symptoms relate to sea level rise and human activities is a significant question for future research at Everglades National Park.

Tree Islands, Hardwood Hammocks, and Rock Ridges

Tree islands and larger hardwood hammocks are unique and prevalent features at Everglades National Park. Their elevated forests dot the sawgrass prairies throughout the park. Bay heads, precursors to hammocks, are tree islands dominated by broad-leaved, evergreen and swamp hardwood species. These areas exist on high peat benches above the surrounding marsh and often develop at solution holes or relative depressions in the solid bedrock. Peat and other organic material accumulate in the depression and nurture the development of larger trees and forests. Peat continues to accumulate until a topographic high is created (fig. 8). If this peat creation continues without loss to fires, hardwood hammocks ultimately develop.

Hardwood Hammocks are a climax community of dense vegetation developed in a long-standing absence of fire. The presence of deeper water and/or high humidity dense vegetation shelters the hammocks from fire danger whereas temperature and salinity changes may limit the development of hardwood hammocks (McPherson et al. 1976). At Everglades National Park, the hammock areas contain some of the rarest and most unusual plant and animal species. Over 100 species of trees and shrubs occur, ranging from red maple and laurel oak trees in the lower hammock areas to live oak and cabbage palm in high parts of the northern hammock areas. To the south, tropical species such as strangler fig, wild tamarind, pigeon plumb, gumbo limbo, poisonwood, coco plum, redbay, and other broad-leaved tropical trees and shrubs dominate the hammocks (McPherson et al. 1976).

The existence and origin of hammocks is dependent upon the underlying geology and geologic processes. Hammock development depends upon having land slightly higher than that of the surrounding marshes and prairies. This higher land supported ancient human occupations as evidenced by pottery fragments, metal containers, and planted exotic species. In south Florida, this elevation difference is usually less than a meter. Hammock development is slow because organic material must build up over many years to create a topographic high (McPherson et al. 1976). Bedrock units may provide a source of phosphorous for the hardwood forests of hammocks, tree islands, and rock ridges, described below. Hydrogeochemical studies are necessary to identify or quantify this relationship.

Spatially, tree islands and hardwood hammocks are oriented in linear trends. The islands and hammocks may be located in bedrock highs or lows. Some believe they develop in peat depressions caused by organic deposition into solution holes, or perhaps on a laminated duracrust formed by phosphorus from evaporites pulled up by the trees in the groundwater.

Locally referred to as rock reefs, rock ridges, such as that at Rock Reef Pass, are subtle, enigmatic linear features on the Everglades landscape. There are approximately 20 rock ridges in south Florida most of which are oriented perpendicular to the prevailing direction of water flow (Hickey personal communication 2005). These ridges trend northwest-southeast and are typically 10–20 km (6–12 mi) long and usually less than 100 m (330 ft) wide. The amount of relief associated with these ridges is small, approximately 0.9–1.5 m (3–5 ft). However, topographic relief is significant in south Florida on the scale of centimeters and the vegetation changes across these ridges and makes them appear more pronounced (fig. 7). The elevated ridges slow the southward flow of surface water, ponding water on their northern sides, and are responsible for significant changes in vegetation on either side of the ridge axis. These features, eight of which are named on USGS topographic maps, are especially evident on aerial photographs of the Everglades (Hickey 2005).

Many theories abound regarding the existence of these features. They may be paleoshores, results of Pleistocene wrench faulting, developed fractures, concentrations of shells in oolite, paleo mudbanks, or the result of differential compaction and fracturing. The uniqueness of these environments makes understanding the origin and nature of their existence important to resource management at Everglades National Park. Studies such as rotary core drilling, well monitoring (for groundwater geochemistry), and subsurface ground penetrating radar surveys (to determine subsurface geologic structures) may shed light on the origin and distribution of these features as well as provide more information about their effects on the hydrogeologic system at Everglades National Park (Hickey 2005).

Hydrogeology

As peat and marl were deposited in a karstic limestone depression during the past 5,000 years, an extensive subtropical wetland ecosystem developed into the current Florida Everglades (Bruno et al. 2003). Until the late 1800s, interconnected wetlands covered approximately 8.9 million acres of south Florida. Of this expanse, over 4 million acres were known as the "River of Grass"—the Everglades. Perhaps the most critical feature of this ecosystem was the gently sloping landscape and its large capacity of long-term water storage. The water flowed very slowly through the system, buffering extreme changes caused by droughts and floods. Understanding this system means understanding the relationship between geology and water flow (FDEP 2005).

Hydrogeology refers to the study of groundwater movement with specific emphasis on its relation to the surrounding geology, modes of movement, and water chemistry (FGS 2005). This study is multifaceted and interdisciplinary combining hydrology, geology, chemistry, physics, biology, mathematics (modeling), and engineering to understand the characteristics of groundwater movement in the complex subsurface.

Groundwater is the most available source of potable water in south Florida. Water-bearing rocks at Everglades National Park include carbonate limestone and dolostone (a rock rich in dolomite). As described above in the karst description, these rocks are heavily dissolved in the subsurface and are highly permeable. Permeability refers to the degree to which water is able to flow freely through a rock (FGS 2005).

When groundwater collects in subsurface zones, it is referred to as an aquifer. A viable aquifer typically yields water in sufficient quantities to support human activities such as agriculture and domestic use. Aquifers are classified as unconfined, semi-confined, or confined based on the physical parameters by which the water is contained in the aquifer. Unconfined aquifers are defined as having the general water table as an upper boundary. These are open to meteoric water filtering through the soil and subsurface and are thus susceptible to pollution from agricultural and domestic use.

A confined aquifer is any water bearing layer that is sandwiched between two aquitards. An aquitard is a layer of rock that is so impermeable it cannot transmit useful amounts of groundwater (IGS 2006). Semi-confined aquifers share characteristics of confined and unconfined aquifers that vary spatially.

The Florida aquifer system contains all three types of aquifers described above. This system underlies all of Florida and is the main source of water for most human use (FGS 2005). This system resides at different stratigraphic levels below the surface. The unconfined Biscayne aquifer, prominent in the Everglades, is comprised of karstic Pleistocene platform carbonates of the Miami Limestone and Fort Thompson Formation (fig. 9) (Cunningham 2004a; Cunningham 2004b)). The high porosity and permeability of these units allows considerable exchange between surface and ground waters (Bruno et al. 2003). Over portions of south Florida, a cap rock cover on the porous limestone exerts control on the surface flow of water and its subsequent infiltration into the groundwater. Cap rock, bedrock structures (pinnacles) and dissolution features such as solution cavities, buried sinkholes, and conduit networks create significant issues for hydrogeologic modeling at the Everglades (Kruse et al. 2000).

With the recent funding of the Comprehensive Everglades Restoration Plan (CERP), innovative and vital research and studies are underway to understand the changes in the natural habitats of the Everglades as a result of human activities. CERP intends to restore natural patterns of water flow and all data related to the hydrogeologic system at Everglades National Park is critical to this goal. This cooperative effort is multi-agency with involvement from the National Park Service, National Oceanic and Atmospheric Association, U.S. Geological Survey, Florida Department of Environmental Protection, South Florida Water Management District, U.S. Army Corps of Engineers, Florida Geologic Survey, South Florida Natural Resources Center, Florida International University, etc. (Loftus et al. 2001; SFWMD 2002).

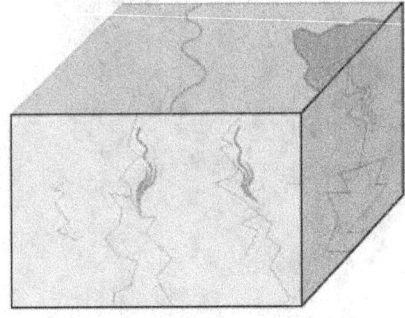

Rainwater and groundwater percolate through underground fissures, dissolving carbonate minerals and creating wider cavities and conduits.

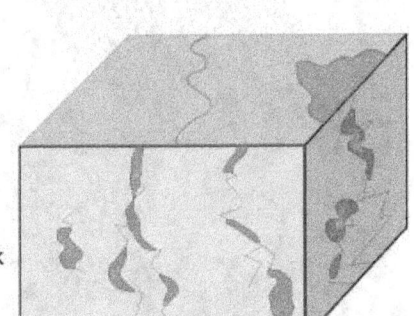

Conduits continue to widen, creating an underground network of cavities.

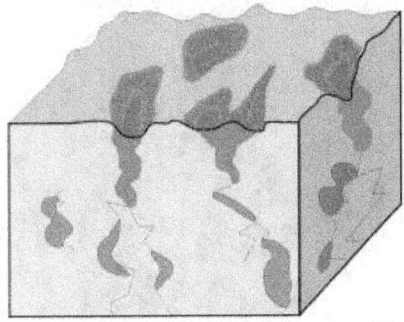

Rocks above cavities and voids collapse to form dissolution holes and sinkholes. Lakes and rivers may disappear underground.

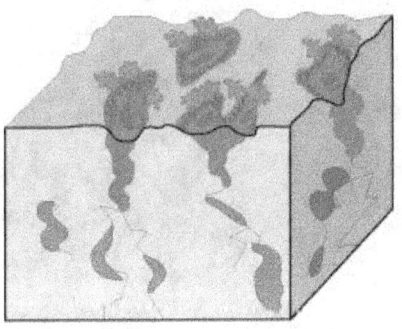

Dissolution holes begin to accumulate peat and organic material, which support cypress and willow.

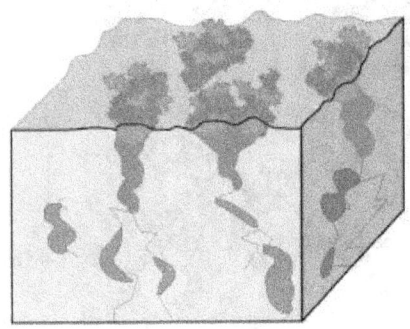

Mixed swamp forest succeeds cypress and willow, eventually resulting in more accumlation of peat and creating a topographic high that will support the hardwood hammock climax forest.

Figure 5: Development of a karst landscape from early dissolution of bedrock to the ultimate formation of a hardwood hammock in the Everglades. Graphic is by Trista L. Thornberry-Ehrlich (Colorado State University).

Figure 6: Solution holes formed by collapse of uppermost rock layer in Everglades National Park. Photographs by Trista L. Thornberry-Ehrlich (Colorado State University).

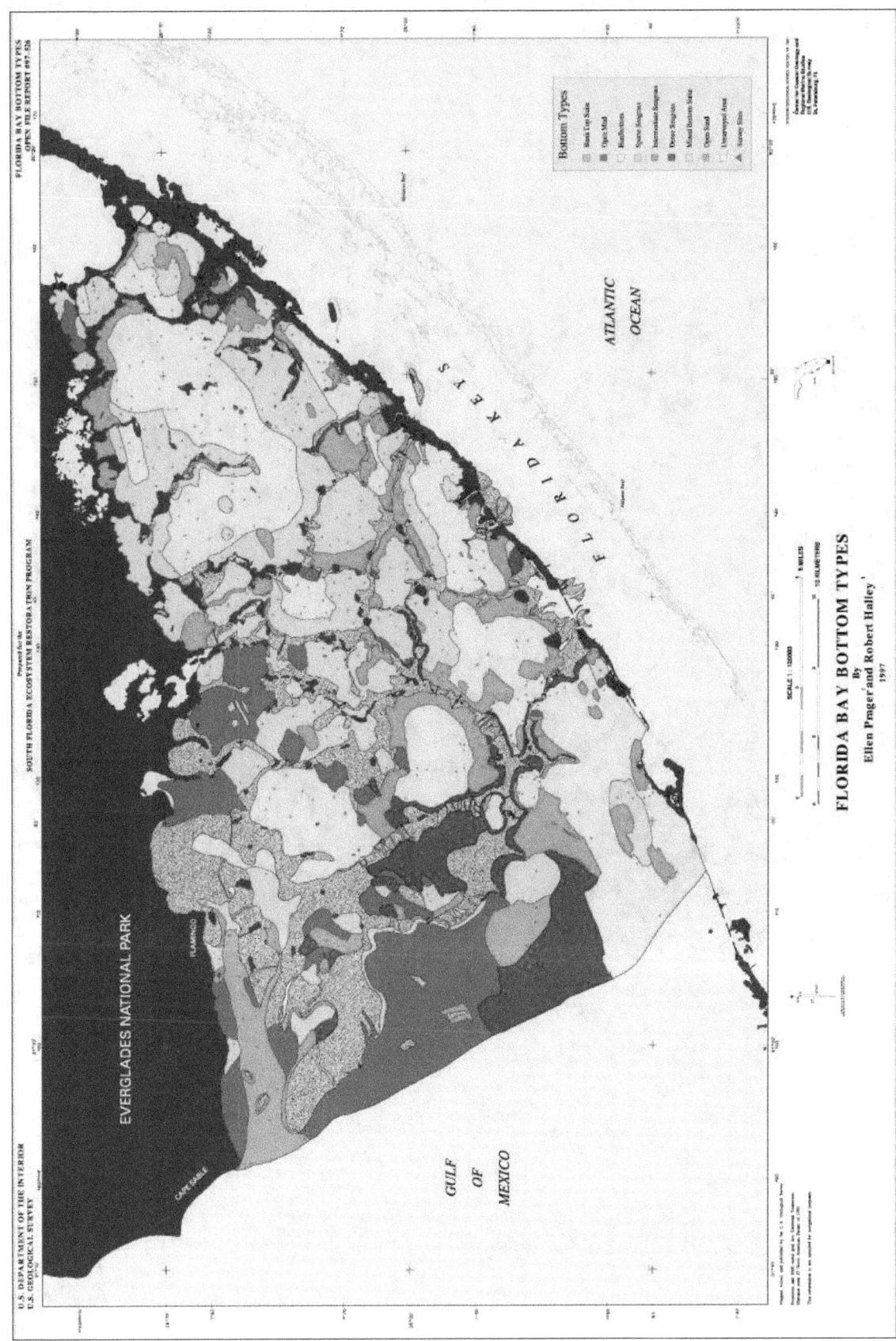

Figure 7: Map of bottom types of Florida Bay. Preliminary map is by the U.S. Geological Survey.

Figure 8: View of a rock ridge (Rock Reef Pass, 1 m [3 ft] of relief) in Everglades National Park. Note vegetation pattern. Photograph is by Trista L. Thornberry-Ehrlich (Colorado State University).

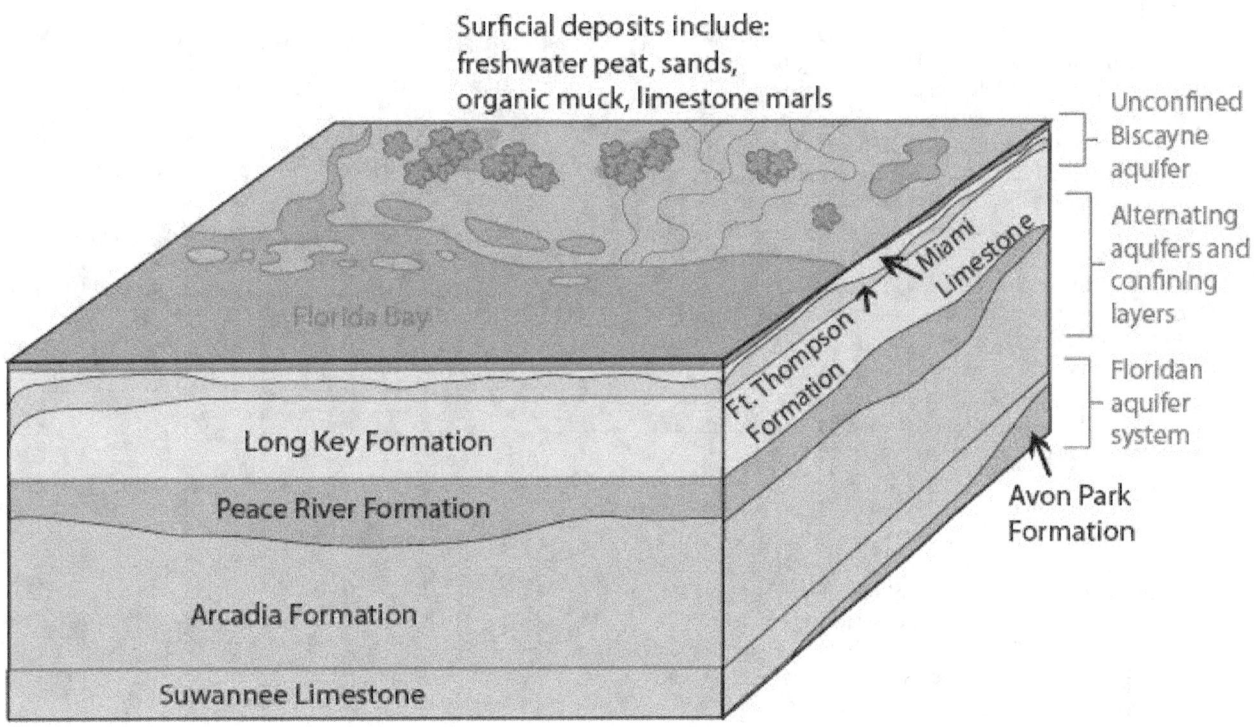

Figure 9: Cross sectional view of south Florida subsurface in the vicinity of Everglades National Park. Note the location of the different aquifer systems (surficial-Biscayne, intermediate, and Floridan systems) and geologic units. Graphic is by Trista L. Thornberry-Ehrlich (Colorado State University) using information from Cunningham (2005) and SFWMD (2002).

Map Unit Properties

This section identifies characteristics of map units that appear on the Geologic Resource Evaluation digital geologic map of Everglades National Park. The accompanying table is highly generalized and is provided for background purposes only. Ground-disturbing activities should not be permitted or denied on the basis of information in this table.

Geologic maps facilitate an understanding of Earth, its processes, and the geologic history responsible for its formation. Hence, the geologic map for Everglades National Park informed the "Geologic History," "Geologic Features and Processes," and "Geologic Issues" sections of this report. Geologic maps are essentially two-dimensional representations of complex three-dimensional relationships. The various colors on geologic maps represent rocks and unconsolidated deposits. Bold lines that cross and separate the color patterns mark structural features such as faults and folds. Point symbols indicate features such as dipping strata, sample localities, mine features, wells, and cave openings.

In serving the conservation and recreation needs of the nation, resource managers consider other resources—water, soils, vegetation, and cultural—in concert with geology. Incorporation of geologic data into a geographic information system (GIS) increases the utility of geologic maps and clarifies spatial relationships to other natural resources and anthropogenic features.

Geologic maps are indicators of water resources because they show which rock units are potential aquifers and are useful for finding seeps and springs. Geologic maps do not show soil types and are not soil maps, but they do show parent material, a key factor in soil formation. Furthermore, resource managers have used geologic maps to make correlations between geology and biology; for instance, geologic maps have served as tools for locating threatened and endangered plant species.

Although geologic maps do not show where future earthquakes will occur, the presence of a fault indicates past movement and possible future seismic activity. Geologic maps will not show where the next landslide, rockfall, or volcanic eruption will occur, but mapped deposits show areas that have been susceptible to such geologic hazards. Geologic maps do not show archaeological or cultural resources, but past peoples may have inhabited or been influenced by various geomorphic features that are shown on geologic maps: alluvial terraces may preserve artifacts, and inhabited alcoves may occur at the contact between two rock units.

The features and properties of the geologic units in the following table correspond to the accompanying digital geologic data. Map units are listed from youngest to oldest. Please refer to the geologic time scale (fig. 10) for the age associated with each time period. This table highlights characteristics of map units such as susceptibility to hazards; the occurrence of fossils, cultural resources, mineral resources, and caves; and the suitability as habitat or for recreational use. The

following are source data for the GRE digital geologic map:

Scott, T. M. 2001. *Geologic Formations of Florida (digital)*. Scale 1:126,720. Open-File Report 80. Tallahassee, Florida: Florida Geological Survey.

Green, R., K. Campbell, and T. Scott. 1996. *Surficial and bedrock geology of the western portion of the USGS 1:100,000 scale Homestead quadrangle*. Scale 1:100,000. Open File Map Series 83/08-12. Tallahassee, Florida: Florida Geological Survey.

Green, R., K. Campbell, and T. Scott. 1995. *Surficial and bedrock geology of the eastern portion of the USGS 1:100,000 scale Homestead quadrangle*. Scale 1:100,000. Open File Map Series 83/01-07. Tallahassee, Florida: Florida Geological Survey.

Green, R., K. Campbell, T. Scott, and G. Means. 1998. *Surficial and bedrock geology of the eastern portion of the USGS 1:100,000 scale Sarasota quadrangle and the western portion of the Arcadia quadrangle*. Scale 1:100,000. Open File Map Series 87. Tallahassee, Florida: Florida Geological Survey.

Green, R., G. Means, T. Scott, J. Arthur, and K. Campbell. 1999. *Surficial and bedrock geology of the eastern portion of the USGS 1:100,000 scale Arcadia quadrangle, south-central Florida*. Scale 1:100,000. Open File Map Series 88. Tallahassee, Florida: Florida Geological Survey.

Green, R., Scott, T., Campbell, K., Arthur, J., and Means, G.H. 1997. *Surficial and bedrock geology of the western portion of the USGS 1:100,000 scale Sarasota quadrangle, south-central Florida*. Scale 1:100,000. Florida Geological Survey Open File Map Series 86. Tallahassee, Florida: Florida Geological Survey.

McCartan, L. and W. Moy. 1995. *Geologic maps of the Sarasota and Arcadia, Florida 30x60-minute quadrangles*. Scale 1:100,000. OF-95-261. Reston, VA: U.S. Geological Survey.

Causaras, C.R. 1985. *Geology of the surficial aquifer system, Broward County, Florida*. Scale 1:134,000.Water-Resources Investigations Report 84. Reston, VA: U.S. Geological Survey.

Causaras, C.R. 1986. Geology of the surficial aquifer system, Dade County, Florida: USGS Water-Resources Investigations Report 86. Reston, VA: U.S. Geological Survey.

Bergendahl, M.H. 1956. *Stratigraphy of parts of De Soto and Hardee Counties, Florida*. Scale 1:158,400. Bulletin 1030-B. Reston, VA: U.S. Geological Survey

Reese, R.S. and K.J. Cunningham. 2000. *Hydrogeology of the gray limestone aquifer in southern Florida.* Scale 1:675,000. Water-Resources Investigations Report 99-4213, Reston, VA: U.S. Geological Survey.

Florida Fish and Wildlife Commission Florida Marine Research Center. 1999. *Benthic Habitats of Florida Bay, FL 1991-1995, CD-ROM.* Scale 1:48,000. National Oceanic and Atmospheric Administration Coastal Services Center.

Yon, J.W., S.M. Spencer, R.W. Hoenstine, and E. Lane. 1988. *Mineral resources of Collier County, Florida.* Scale 1:126,720. Map Series 120. Tallahassee, Florida: Florida Geological Survey.

Lane, E., T.M. Scott, R.W. Hoenstine, and J.W. Yon. 1990. *Mineral resources of Lee County, Florida.* Scale 1:126,720. Map Series 130. Tallahassee, Florida: Florida Geological Survey.

Arthur, J.D., A.E. Baker, J.R. Cichon, A.R. Wood, and A. Rudin. 2005. *Florida Aquifer Vulnerability Assessment (FAVA): Contamination potential of Florida's principal aquifer systems.* Florida Geological Survey Bulletin [in review]. Tallahassee, Florida: Florida Geological Survey.

Using ESRI ArcGIS software, the Geologic Resource Evaluation team created a digital geologic map from this source. GRE digital geologic-GIS map products include data in ESRI shapefile and coverage GIS formats, FGDC metadata, a Windows HelpFile that contains all of the ancillary map information and graphics, and an ESRI ArcMap map document file that easily displays the map with appropriate symbology.

GRE digital geologic data are included on the attached CD and are available through the NPS Data Store (http://science.nature.nps.gov/nrdata/).

Everglades National Park Geologic Map Unit Notes

The topographic relief in Everglades National Park is slight and only a few distinct units are revealed at the surface. Cores such as the deep, continuous core near the Everglades National Park Research Center (W-17232), those of the South Florida Drilling Project (Florida Geological Survey, University of Miami, Florida Department of Transportation), and the USGS help define the stratigraphy underlying the park. This stratigraphy includes carbonate-clastic and evaporite units that have been accumulating for millions of years.

The lowest unit penetrated by the W-17232 core in the park is the Arcadia Formation (top surface at 147 m [482 ft] below the ground surface). As mapped, the Arcadia Formation is exposed on the southwestern flank of the Ocala Platform from Pasco County southward to Sarasota County in the northwestern portion of the park (Scott 2001). The Suwannee Limestone and Avon Park Formation (not penetrated by the W-17232 core) underlie this unit in Everglades National Park.

A major disconformity marks the boundary between the Arcadia Formation and the overlying Peace River Formation. The Peace River Formation contains two distinct units: a lower diatomaceous mudstone, and an upper fine-grained quartz muddy sandstone (Cunningham et al. 1998). The Bone Valley Member of the Peace River Formation occurs in a limited area in Hillsborough, Polk, and Hardee Counties and contains unique phosphatic deposits (Scott 2001). The Peace River Formation unit pinches out south of Everglades National Park. The top of the Peace River Formation is 98.8 m (324 ft) below the surface at W-17232 (McNeill et al. 1996). In the western areas of south Florida, the Pliocene carbonate-siliciclastic Tamiami Formation is exposed atop the Peace River Formation.

Cunningham et al. (1998) proposed a new unit, the Long Key Formation, for subsurface siliciclastics underlying the southernmost reaches of Florida (from core W-17156 on Long Key). This unit is coeval with the Stock Island Formation of the lower Florida Keys and the Cypresshead Formation of the peninsula (Guertin et al. 1999; Scott 2001). The top of the Long Key Formation in the park is 17.4 m (57 ft) below the surface. The siliciclastics of the unit were deposited in at least three high-energy pulses. They are present in a channelized morphology of coarse-grained sands (>1 mm) (Warzeski et al. 1996). Other Tertiary map units in the park area include dunes, and shell-bearing sediments (Scott 2001).

Shallow water limestone of the Fort Thompson Formation comprises the uppermost 17 m (55 ft) of cored section in the Everglades. This limestone is locally combined with the capping unit of the Miami Limestone. The Fort Thomson Formation grades laterally into the Key Largo Limestone to the east and west of the park (Cunningham 2005). The Fort Thompson Formation is mostly lagoonal facies carbonate with abundant bivalve fossils and some quartz sand. The Miami Limestone is 125–130 thousand years old and records interglacial deposition.

Overlying the Miami Limestone bedrock are surficial units of beach ridge and dunes, freshwater peat and organic muck, freshwater and marine marls, thin soils, and cyanobacteria mats (Scott 2001: Cunningham 2005). The peat and muck typically occur in low-lying sloughs and solution holes and are dark and fine-grained. During the standing water phase of the wet season, extracellular precipitation of calcium carbonate by cyanobacteria forms fresh and marine limestone marls. The marine marls (Flamingo Marl) are dominated by aragonitic (calcium carbonate) mud, and shell deposits that form a sort of coastal levee around the southern rim of the park (Cunningham 2005).

Map units for Everglades National Park also include benthic habitats in Florida Bay as captured by aerial photogrammetry. Unconsolidated units include sand banks, sand, mixed fine seagrass areas, mud banks, and dredged muds. Some habitats were also delineated based on the degree of submerged aquatic vegetation and submerged rooted vascular plant cover. This cover ranged from non-existent, discontinuous, and dredged to continuous. Other habitats surveyed include land, reef, seagrass, and hardbottom types (FFWC 1999).

Geologic History

This section describes the rocks and unconsolidated deposits that appear on the digital geologic map of Everglades National Park, the environment in which those units were deposited, and the timing of geologic events that created the present landscape.

The Florida platform is among the younger additions to the North American continent. Thousands of meters of interlayered carbonates and siliciclastics represent a predominantly stable depositional environment punctuated by erosional and high-energy events. The rocks deep below Florida give clues to its origin and geologic history (fig. 10).

Late Paleozoic Era

During the Mississippian, the landmass that now underlies the grand carbonate platform of Florida was not attached to the North American craton. It may have been attached to the northwest portion of the African continent (Condie and Sloan 1998). In any case, marine carbonates were deposited over large portions of the area atop a Paleozoic age crystalline basement high, the Peninsular Arch (Pollastro et al. 2000).

In the Pennsylvanian, a collision event, known as the Ouachita orogeny sutured the Florida landmass to the continent as Gondwanaland and North America collided. This plate movement eventually formed the supercontinent Pangaea. Many north to northeast trending strike-slip and thrust faults were active, as a result of the multi-directional tectonic stresses at this time (Amsbury and Haenggi 1993). South Florida was completely submerged and located at the junction of the North American, South American, and African plates (fig. 11). Through the Permian, Pangaea remained intact (Condie and Sloan 1998). Highlands to the north of the Florida landmass eroded quickly when compressional tectonic forces subsided during the Permian.

Early Mesozoic Era

At the beginning of the Triassic Period, Pangaea began to break up (~220–245 Ma). During the late Triassic–Jurassic periods, South and Central America and Africa began to rift away from North America. This established the long-standing passive margin of the eastern seaboard that persists today. The Florida and Cuba blocks detached from northwest Africa and the Gulf of Mexico opened (Condie and Sloan 1998). This created large basins for deposition of sediments shed from the rapidly eroding Ouachitan highlands. In the early stages, a series of discontinuous rift basins developed parallel to the edge of the opening ocean basin. These basins extended from Mexico to Nova Scotia (Hentz 2001).

Accompanying the rifting of Pangaea was the widespread extrusion of volcanic rocks consistent with mantle plume upwelling due to crustal tension (Heatherington and Mueller 1991). This continental rifting also opened the Atlantic Ocean basin.

Middle Mesozoic Era

Underlying the south Florida basin are igneous rhyolitic–basaltic rocks (Thomas et al. 1989). These rocks were sampled from a 5.7 km (3.5 mi) deep core in Collier County. Geochemical composition indicates they were formed within a mantle plume in a continental rifting environment consistent with the breakup of Pangaea. Geologists surmise a hotspot initiated local rifting off the southern tip of the Florida Platform (Heatherington and Mueller 1991; Cunningham 2005).

These igneous rocks were subaerially exposed and eroded during the late Triassic to middle Jurassic. Deposits of sands and silts covered local areas, which upon exposure formed redbeds. Accompanying the opening of the proto-Atlantic Ocean, the Caribbean basin, and the ancestral Gulf of Mexico were major lateral displacements along transform faults such as the North Bahamas fracture zone (Condie and Sloan 1998).

During the late Jurassic the Atlantic Ocean and Caribbean basin continued to develop, depositing deltaic and shallow marine sediments over the Florida Platform. Restriction of marine circulation at this time resulted in periodic accumulations of evaporites and marine carbonates (Cunningham 2005). Deposition of Jurassic and Cretaceous sediments was controlled by the south-southeast plunging axis of the Peninsular Arch. Basal sediments onlap and pinch out against the arch (Pollastro et al. 2000).

Late Mesozoic Era

As sea level rise proceeded during the early Cretaceous, the Florida Platform was the site of more widespread deposition of marine limestones and reefs. Reef distribution was clustered along the margin of the ancestral Gulf of Mexico and the edges of the Florida Platform (Cunningham 2005). From the Middle Cretaceous to the Late Paleogene, the Suwannee Strait (often called the Gulf Trough) separated the carbonate Florida Platform from a clastic shelf and slope that was developing along the southeastern margin of North America. These clastics originated from the eroding Appalachian Mountains. Currents running through the strait prevented the clastics from interrupting the continuous accumulation of carbonates on the Florida platform. As currents changed and the seaway was infilled, by the late Eocene, some of the siliciclastics were mixed with the deep carbonate sediments (Cunningham et al. 2003).

Further transgression and global warming during the Late Cretaceous established an open marine accumulation of carbonates over the entire Florida Peninsula. Accompanying this widespread accumulation was the development of reefal deposition of rudistid bivalves around the southern margin of the Florida area.

By the Late Cretaceous, the Gulf of Mexico was completely open. The new crust formed by igneous extrusion during extension was now the Proto-Caribbean tectonic plate. This oceanic crust separates the Gulf of Mexico and the Yucatan from South America. At this time, the Antilles arc (portions of which now comprise parts of Hispaniola and Puerto Rico) moved eastward and began subducting beneath the Cuba Block (Condie and Sloan 1998).

Cenozoic Era

Cenozoic development of the Florida Platform included additional deposition of marine carbonates and deposition of siliciclastics from northwestern highlands sources and long shore oceanic currents. Tertiary faulting occurred south of Florida as the Cuban block continued to collide with the Antilles arc and carbonate accumulation continued in Florida (Condie and Sloan 1998). In southern Florida, the open marine depositional setting continued during the Paleocene as more restricted flow to the north resulted in deposits of mixed carbonates and intermittent evaporites (during restricted marine conditions). Eocene and Oligocene deposition is marked by shallow water carbonates. Intermittent with this deposition were subaerial exposures forming erosional surfaces and scant redbeds associated with local oceanic regressions.

Deposition in south Florida during the Miocene changed with the introduction of more widespread siliciclastics from a fluvio-deltaic system prograding down the peninsula. These deposits were derived from the rapidly eroding southern Appalachian Mountains as the Atlantic Coastal Plain physiographic province continued to develop eastward. Phosphates and the carbonate ramp of the Arcadia Formation were deposited during the Miocene in southeastern Florida (Cunningham 2005). Siliciclastic deposits comprising the Peace River Formation then buried this carbonate ramp in the Miocene. Marine upwelling at this time is responsible for the diatomaceous mudstones and high organic productivity represented by the lower beds of the Peace River Formation (Cunningham et al. 1998).

Some of the Miocene siliciclastic deposits of the Peace River Formation were eroded and reworked during a marine regression. This Pliocene lowstand caused a disconformity between the Peace River and overlying Long Key Formation. South of Everglades National Park, the Peace River Formation is absent – either never deposited or eroded away completely. During the Pliocene, the Everglades area was the focus of deposition of a thick pile of sand eroded from the Miocene deposits that was being transported south to eventually form the Long Key Formation (Guertin et al. 1999; Cunningham 2005). This wedge of sand covered the area that is now Everglades National Park and extended as far south as the Florida Keys. Deposition was in fluctuating outer and inner shelf conditions with depths ranging from 150–180 m (~500–600 ft) to 10–50 m (~30–150 ft), respectively (Guertin et al. 1999).

In addition to Pliocene siliciclastic deposition, local carbonate accumulations also occurred in south Florida. In the western reaches of the peninsula, was a mid-Pliocene reef environment. Near the lower Florida Keys and the southwest Florida shelf, the coeval carbonates of the Stock Island Formation were deposited. These sediments were perhaps associated with currents originating in the Gulf of Mexico, flowing eastward through the Straits of Florida (Cunningham et al. 1998; Cunningham 2005).

The Pleistocene Epoch is known for numerous extensive glacial events, which alternated with warmer interglacial stages. Although glacial ice never extended as far south as Florida, the accompanying global-scale climatic and sea level shifts played a major role in the formation of the geologic units and the overall landscape exposed today at Everglades National Park. The Pleistocene resulted in the conversion from siliciclastic deposition mixed with carbonate accumulation to more widespread carbonate sedimentation with occasional, localized siliciclastic contributions (Cunningham 2005). Global sea-level changes during the intermittent glacial/interglacial stages of the Pleistocene controlled the rate and distribution of carbonate units.

During the last interglacial period (120–130 thousand years), mixed carbonate-siliciclastic sediments formed the Fort Thompson Formation. Deposition occurred in a restricted lagoonal environment (rich in marine fossil remains) during minor fluctuations in sea level. This unit interfingers with the surficial geologic units, the Miami and Key Largo Limestones, and the Anastasia Formation (~130 thousand years) (Cunningham 2005).

The eastern areas of Everglades National Park contain exposures of the oolitic facies of the Miami Limestone. This unit is comprised of oolitic and pelloidal carbonate sands. These deposits grade westward into a lower energy, more restricted, bryozoan facies of the unit. Throughout the park area, the surface exposures of Miami Limestone contain a mixture of bryozoan remains, ooids, and lime peloids (Cunningham 2005).

Sea level began to rise rapidly 15–16 thousand years ago and by 6–7 thousand years ago southern Florida was extensively flooded (Shinn et al. 1997). Since that time sea level has continued to rise. Holocene geologic activity in the Everglades area consists of the pervasive dissolution of carbonate bedrock units, the surficial accumulation of carbonate muds, marine and freshwater marls, sands, and swamp deposits. Holocene sediment distribution is controlled by the geology, sea level, climate, and vegetation patterns (Cunningham 2005).

In lower sloughs and solution holes, deposition of organic muck and peat soils dominates (Craighead 1971). Freshwater marl and cyanobacteria mats dominate the open prairies and deeper sloughs where calcium carbonate precipitates *in situ* covering the ground and vegetation (fig. 12). Marine marls dominate the coastal areas of Florida Bay. Flood events are responsible for the formation of these natural levees composed of aragonitic mud and shell fragments (Cunningham 2005).

Eon	Era	Period	Epoch	Ma	Life Forms	N. American Tectonics
Phanerozoic (Phaneros = "evident"; zoic = "life")	Cenozoic	Quaternary	Holocene	0.01	Age of Mammals: Modern humans	Cascade volcanoes (W)
			Pleistocene		Extinction of large mammals and birds	Worldwide glaciation
				1.8		
		Tertiary	Pliocene		Large carnivores	Uplift of Sierra Nevada (W)
				5.3	Whales and apes	Linking of N. and S. America
			Miocene	23.0		
			Oligocene			Basin-and-Range extension (W)
				33.9		
			Eocene	55.8	Early primates	Laramide Orogeny ends (W)
			Paleocene			
				65.5		
	Mesozoic	Cretaceous			Age of Dinosaurs: Mass extinction / Placental mammals / Early flowering plants	Laramide Orogeny (W) / Sevier Orogeny (W) / Nevadan Orogeny (W)
				145.5		
		Jurassic			First mammals	Elko Orogeny (W)
				199.6	Mass extinction	Breakup of Pangaea begins
		Triassic			Flying reptiles / First dinosaurs	Sonoma Orogeny (W)
				251		
	Paleozoic	Permian			Age of Amphibians: Mass extinction / Coal-forming forests diminish	Supercontinent Pangaea intact / Ouachita Orogeny (S) / Alleghenian (Appalachian) Orogeny (E)
				299		Ancestral Rocky Mts. (W)
		Pennsylvanian			Coal-forming swamps / Sharks abundant / Variety of insects	
				318.1	First amphibians	
		Mississippian			First reptiles	Antler Orogeny (W)
				359.2	Mass extinction	
		Devonian			Fishes: First forests (evergreens)	Acadian Orogeny (E-NE)
				416		
		Silurian			First land plants	
				443.7	Mass extinction	
		Ordovician			Marine Invertebrates: First primitive fish / Trilobite maximum / Rise of corals	Taconic Orogeny (NE)
				488.3		Avalonian Orogeny (NE)
		Cambrian			Early shelled organisms	Extensive oceans cover most of N. America
				542		
Proterozoic ("Early life")		Precambrian			First multicelled organisms	Formation of early supercontinent / Grenville Orogeny (E)
				2500	Jellyfish fossil (670 Ma)	First iron deposits / Abundant carbonate rocks
Archean ("Ancient")				≈4000	Early bacteria and algae	Oldest known Earth rocks (≈3.96 billion years ago)
Hadean ("Beneath the Earth")					Origin of life?	Oldest moon rocks (4-4.6 billion years ago)
				4600		Earth's crust being formed

Formation of the Earth

Figure 10: Geologic time scale; adapted from the U.S. Geological Survey (http://pubs.usgs.gov/fs/2007/3015/). Red lines indicate major unconformities between eras. Included are major events in life history and tectonic events occurring on the North American continent. Absolute ages shown are in millions of years.

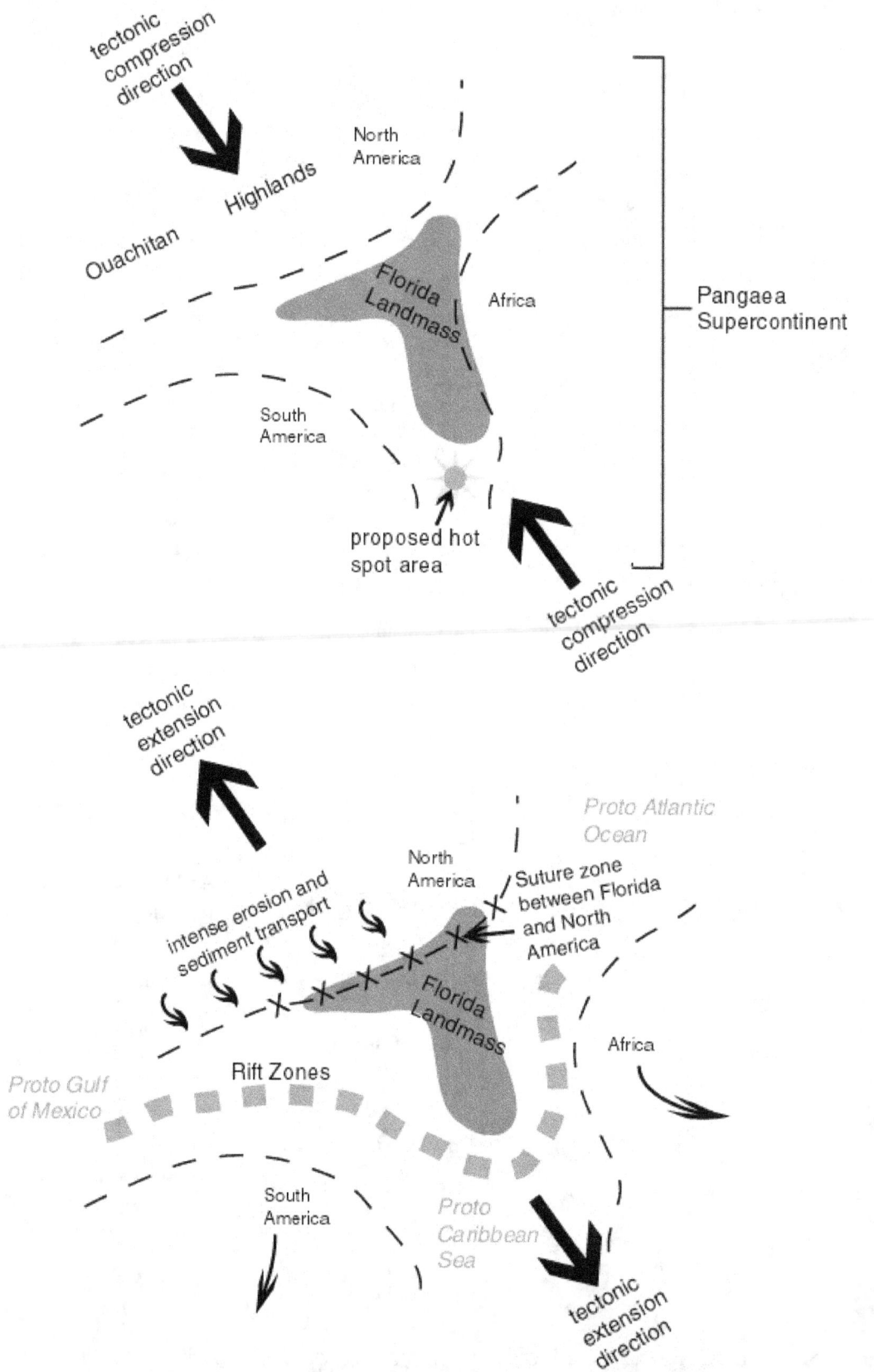

Figure 11: Evolution of the landscape in the Florida Platform area from the Mississippian-Pennsylvanian Ouachita orogeny through the Triassic-Jurassic extensional event opening the Gulf of Mexico, the Caribbean Sea, and the Atlantic Ocean. The Florida landmass sutured to the North American continent at this time. Diagram is not to scale. Graphic is by Trista L. Thornberry-Ehrlich (Colorado State University).

Figure 12: Freshwater limestone marl coating the surface of the ground and vegetation in a open prairie area at Everglades National Park. Photograph is by Trista L. Thornberry-Ehrlich (Colorado State University).

Glossary

This glossary contains brief definitions of technical geologic terms used in this report. Not all geologic terms used are referenced. For more detailed definitions or to find terms not listed here please visit: http://wrgis.wr.usgs.gov/docs/parks/misc/glossarya.html.

aquifer. Rock or sediment that is sufficiently porous, permeable, and saturated to be useful as a source of water.

aragonitic. Pertaining to the mineral aragonite ($CaCO_3$).

asthenosphere. Weak layer in the upper mantle below the lithosphere where seismic waves are attenuated.

axis (fold). A straight line approximation that when moved parallel to itself generates the shape of a fold (see and use hingeline)

barchan dune. A crescent-shaped dune with arms or horns of the crescent pointing downwind. The crescent or barchan type is most characteristic of the inland desert regions.

barrier island. A long, low, narrow island formed by a ridge of sand that parallels the coast.

basement. The undifferentiated rocks, commonly igneous and metamorphic, that underlie the rocks of interest.

basin (structural). A doubly-plunging syncline in which rocks dip inward from all sides.

basin (sedimentary). Any depression, from continental to local scales, into which sediments are deposited.

beach. A gently sloping shoreline covered with sediment, often formed by action of waves and tides.

bed. The smallest sedimentary strata unit, commonly ranging in thickness from one centimeter to a meter or two and distinguishable from beds above.

bedding. Depositional layering or stratification of sediments.

calcareous. A rock or sediment containing calcium carbonate.

cementation. Chemical precipitation of material into pores between grains that bind the grains into rock.

chemical sediment. A sediment precipitated directly from solution (also called nonclastic).

chemical weathering. The dissolution or chemical breakdown of minerals at Earth's surface via reaction with water, air, or dissolved substances.

clastic. Rock or sediment made of fragments or pre-existing rocks.

clay. Clay minerals or sedimentary fragments the size of clay minerals (<2 cm).

conglomerate. A coarse-grained sedimentary rock with clasts larger than 2 mm in a fine-grained matrix.

continental crust. The type of crustal rocks underlying the continents and continental shelves; having a thickness of 25–60 km (16–37 mi) and a density of approximately 2.7 grams per cubic centimeter.

continental rise. Gently sloping region from the foot of the continental slope to the abyssal plain.

continental shelf. The shallowly-submerged portion of a continental margin extending from the shoreline to the continental slope with water depths of less than 200 m (656 ft).

continental slope. The relative steep slope from the outer edge of the continental shelf down to the more gently sloping ocean depths of the continental rise or abyssal plain.

convergent boundary. A plate boundary where two tectonic plates are moving together (i.e., a zone of subduction or obduction).

craton. The relatively old and geologically stable interior of a continent.

cross-bedding. Uniform to highly-varied sets of inclined sedimentary beds deposited by wind or water that indicate distinctive flow conditions.

cross section. A graphical interpretation of geology, structure, and/or stratigraphy in the third (vertical) dimension based on mapped and measured geological extents and attitudes depicted in an oriented vertical plane.

crust. The outermost compositional shell of Earth, 10–40 km (6–25 mi) thick, consisting predominantly of relatively low-density silicate minerals (also see oceanic crust and continental crust).

crystalline. Describes the structure of a regular, orderly, repeating geometric arrangement of atoms

deformation. A general term for the process of faulting, folding, shearing, extension, or compression of rocks as a result of various Earth forces.

delta. A sediment wedge deposited at a stream's mouth where it flows into a lake or sea.

dip. The angle between a structural surface and a horizontal reference plane measured normal to their line of intersection.

disconformity. An unconformity at which the bedding of the strata above and below are parallel.

divergent boundary. A tectonic plate boundary where the plates are moving apart (e.g., a spreading ridge or continental rift zone).

dune. A low mound or ridge of sediment, usually sand, deposited by wind. Common dune types include the barchan dune, longitudinal dune, parabolic dune, and transverse dune (see respective listings).

eolian. Formed, eroded, or deposited by or related to the action of the wind.

estuary. The seaward end or tidal mouth of a river where fresh and sea water mix. Many estuaries are drowned river valleys caused by sea level rise (transgression) or coastal subsidence.

evaporite. Chemically precipitated mineral(s) formed by the evaporation of solute-rich water under restricted conditions.

facies (sedimentary). The depositional or environmental conditions reflected in the sedimentary structures, textures, mineralogy, fossils, etc. of a sedimentary rock.

fault. A subplanar break in rock along which relative movement occurs between the two sides.

formation. Fundamental rock-stratigraphic unit that is mappable and lithologically distinct from adjoining strata and has definable upper and lower contacts.

fracture. Irregular breakage of a mineral; also any break in a rock (e.g., crack, joint, fault)

igneous. Refers to a rock or mineral that originated from molten material that is one of the three main classes or rocks—igneous, metamorphic, and sedimentary.

joint. A semi-planar break in rock without relative movement of rocks on either side of the fracture surface.

karst topography. Topography characterized by abundant sinkholes and caverns formed by the dissolution of calcareous rocks.

lacustrine. Pertaining to, produced by, or inhabiting a lake or lakes.

levees. Raised ridges lining the banks of a stream; may be natural or artificial.

lineament. Any relatively straight surface feature that can be identified via observation, mapping, or remote sensing, often representing tectonic features.

lithification. The conversion of sediment into solid rock.

lithology. The description of a rock or rock unit, especially the texture, composition, and structure of sedimentary rocks.

lithosphere. The relatively rigid outmost shell of Earth's structure, 50 to 100 km (31 to 62 mi) thick that encompasses the crust and uppermost mantle.

longitudinal dunes. Dunes elongated parallel to the direction of wind flow.

longshore current. A current parallel to a coastline caused by waves approaching the shore at an oblique angle.

mantle. The zone of the Earth's interior between crust and core.

marl. A loose earthy deposit made up of a mixture of clay and calcium carbonate, formed under marine or freshwater conditions.

matrix. The fine-grained interstitial material between coarse grains in porphyritic igneous rocks and poorly sorted clastic sediments or rocks.

mechanical weathering. The physical breakup of rocks without change in composition (syn: physical weathering).

member. A lithostratigraphic unit with definable contacts that subdivides a formation.

obduction. The process by which the crust is thickened by thrust faulting at a convergent margin.

oceanic crust. Earth's crust formed at spreading ridges that underlies the ocean basins. Oceanic crust is 6–7 km (3–4 mi) thick and generally of basaltic composition.

ooid. A small, spheroidal, layered sedimentary grain, usually composed of calcium carbonate. Ooids usually form on the sea floor, most commonly in shallow tropical seas.

orogeny. A mountain-building event, particularly a well-recognized event in the geological past (e.g. the Ouachita orogeny).

outcrop. Any part of a rock mass or formation that is exposed or "crops out" at Earth's surface.

paleontology. The study of the life and chronology of Earth's geologic past based on the phylogeny of fossil organisms.

paleosol. A preserved soil that formed on a landscape in the past with distinctive features resulting from an environment that no longer exists at the site.

Pangaea. A theoretical, single supercontinent that existed during the Permian and Triassic Periods (also see Laurasia and Gondwana).

parabolic dunes. Crescent-shaped dunes with horns or arms that point upwind.

parent (rock). The original rock from which a metamorphic rock or soil was formed.

passive margin. A tectonically quiet continental margin indicated by little volcanic or seismic activity.

pebble. Generally, small, rounded, rock particles from 4 to 64 mm in diameter.

permeability. A measure of the ease or rate that fluids move through rocks or sediments.

plate tectonics. The theory that the lithosphere is broken up into a series of rigid plates that move over Earth's surface above a more fluid asthenosphere.

porosity. The proportion of void space (cracks, interstices) in a volume of a rock or sediment.

regression. A long-term seaward retreat of the shoreline or relative fall of sea level.

rift basin. A depression formed by grabens along the crest of an oceanic spreading ridge or in a continental rift zone.

sandstone. Clastic sedimentary rock of predominantly sand-sized grains.

sediment. An eroded and deposited, unconsolidated accumulation of lithic and mineral fragments.

sedimentary rock. A consolidated and lithified rock consisting of detrital and/or chemical sediment(s).

sequence. A major informal rock-stratigraphic unit that is traceable over large areas and defined by a major sea level transgression-regression sediment package.

siliciclastics. Pertaining to clastic noncarbonated rocks composed almost exclusively of quartz (or other silicate) grains.

silt. Clastic sedimentary material intermediate in size between fine-grained sand and coarse clay (1/256–1/16 mm).

siltstone. A variable-lithified sedimentary rock with silt-sized grains.

slope. The inclined surface of any geomorphic feature or rational measurement thereof (syn: gradient).

soil. Surface accumulation of weathered rock and organic matter capable of supporting plant growth and often overlying the parent rock from which it formed.

spring. A site where water flows out at the surface due to the water table intersecting the ground surface.

strata. Tabular or sheetlike masses or distinct layers (e.g., of rock).

stratigraphy. The geologic study of the origin, occurrence, distribution, classification, correlation, age, etc. of rock layers, especially sedimentary rocks.

strike. The compass direction of the line of intersection that an inclined surface makes with a horizontal plane.

strike-slip fault. A fault with measurable offset where the relative movement is parallel to the strike of the fault.

subduction zone. A convergent plate boundary where oceanic lithosphere descends beneath a continental or oceanic plate and is carried down into the mantle.

subsidence. The gradual sinking or depression of part of Earth's surface.

suture. The linear zone where two continental landmasses become joined due to obduction.

tectonic. Relating to large-scale movement and deformation of Earth's crust.

terraces (stream). Step-like benches surrounding the present floodplain of a stream due to dissection of previous flood plain(s), stream bed(s), and/or valley floor(s).

terrestrial. Relating to Earth or Earth's dry land.

thrust fault. A contractional, dip-slip fault with a shallowly dipping fault surface (<45°) where the hanging wall moves up and over relative to the footwall.

topography. The general morphology of Earth's surface including relief and location of natural and anthropogenic features.

transgression. Landward migration of the sea due to a relative rise in sea level.

transverse dunes. Dunes elongated perpendicular to the prevailing wind direction. The leeward slope stands at or near the angle of repose of sand whereas the windward slope is comparatively gentle.

trend. The direction or azimuth of elongation or a linear geological feature.

unconformity. A surface within sedimentary strata that marks a prolonged period of nondeposition or erosion.

volcanic. Related to volcanoes; describes igneous rock crystallized at or near Earth's surface (e.g., lava).

water table. The upper surface of the saturated (phreatic) zone.

weathering. The set of physical, chemical, and biological processes by which rock is broken down in place.

References

This section lists references cited in this report as well as a general bibliography that may be of use to resource managers. A more complete geologic bibliography is available from the National Park Service Geologic Resources Division.

Amsbury, D. L., W. T. Haenggi. 1993. Middle Pennsylvanian strike-slip faulting in the Llano Uplift, central Texas. *Bulletin of the South Texas Geological Society* 34 (1): 9-16.

Bosence, D. W. J. 1995. Anatomy of a Recent biodetrital mud-mound, Florida Bay, USA. *Special Publications of the International Association of Sedimentologists* 23: 475-493.

Brewster-Wingard, L. 2001. *Ecosystem History: Florida Bay and the Southwest Coast*. U.S. Geological Survey. http://sofia.usgs.gov/projects/eh_fbswc/ (accessed February 28, 2006).

Brooks, H. K. 1981. *Physiographic Divisions map of Florida*. University of Florida Institute of Food and Agricultural Sciences, Center for Environmental and Natural Resources.

Bruno, M. C., K. J. Cunningham, S. A. Perry. 2003. Copepod Communities from Surface and Ground Waters in the Everglades, South Florida. *Southeastern Naturalist* 2(4): 523-546.

Condie, K. C., R. E. Sloan. 1998. Origin and Evolution of the Earth, Principles of Historical Geology. Prentice-Hall, Inc.

Craighead, F. C., Sr. 1971. The Trees of South Florida, Vol. 1, The Natural Environment and their Succession. Coral Gables, FL: University of Miami Press.

Crisfield, E., D. Greco, M. Martin, L. York. 2005. Memorandum re: December 13-15-2004 Site Visit – Evaluation of Restoration Alternatives for the Cape Sable Canals at Everglades National Park (EVER). National Park Service, unpublished.

Cunningham, K. J. 2005. Hydrogeologic Fieldtrip Everglades National Park, Southeastern Florida, unpublished.

Cunningham, K. J. 2004a. Application of ground-penetrating radar, digital optical borehole images, and cores for characterization of porosity hydraulic conductivity and paleokarst in the Biscayne aquifer, southeastern Florida, USA. *Journal of Applied Geophysics* 55: 61-76.

Cunningham, K. J. 2004b. New method for quantification of vuggy porosity from digital optical borehole images as applied to the karstic Pleistocene limestone of the Biscayne aquifer, southeastern Florida. *Journal of Applied Geophysics* 55: 77-90.

Cunningham, K. J., S. D. Locker, A. C. Hine, D. Burky, J. A. Barron, L. A. Guertin. 2003. Interplay of Late Cenozoic Siliciclastic Supply and Carbonate Response on the Southeast Florida Platform. *Journal of Sedimentary Research* 73 (1): 31-46.

Cunningham, K. J., D. F. McNeill, L. A. Guertin, P. F. Ciesielski, T. M. Scott, L. de Verteuil. 1998. New Tertiary Stratigraphy for the Florida Keys and Southern Peninsula of Florida. *Geological Society of America Bulletin* 110: 231-258.

FDEP. 2005. *About the Everglades*. Florida Department of Environmental Protection. http://www.dep.state.fl.us/secretary/ps/default.htm (accessed February 20, 2008).

FFWC. 1999. *Benthic Habitats of Florida Bay, FL 1991-1995*. Florida Fish and Wildlife Commission Florida Marine Research Center – National Oceanic and Atmospheric Administration Coastal Services Center. CD-ROM 1:48,000.

FGS. 2005. *Sinkholes*. Florida Geological Survey, Florida Department of Environmental Protection. http://www.dep.state.fl.us/geology/geologictopics/sinkhole.htm (accessed February 24, 2006).

FLNHM. 2006. *Florida Bay*. Florida Museum of Natural History. http://www.flmnh.ufl.edu/fish/southflorida/FloridaBay.html (accessed February 28, 2006)

Guertin, L. A., D. F. McNeill, B. H. Lidz, K. J. Cunningham. 1999. Chronology and Transgressive/Regressive Signatures in the Late Neogene Siliciclastic Foundation (Long Key Formation) of the Florida Keys. *Journal of Sedimentary Research* 69: 653-666.

Heatherington, A. L., P. A. Mueller. 1991. Geochemical evidence for Triassic rifting in southwestern Florida. *Tectonophysics* 188:291-302.

Hentz, T. F. 2001. Geology. In: *The handbook of Texas. University of Texas at Austin*, http://www.tsha.utexas.edu/handbook/online/articles/GG/swgqz.html (accessed February 28, 2006).

Hickey, D. 2005. Rock Reef Pass – the Mystery of the Rock Ridges. In *Hydrogeologic Fieldtrip Everglades National Park, Southeastern Florida*, Cunningham, K.J. unpublished.

Hoffmeister, J. E., K. W. Stockman, H. G. Multer. 1967. Miami Limestone of Florida and its recent Bahamian counterpart. *Geological Society of America Bulletin* 78: 175-190.

Hoffmeister, J. E. 1974. *Land from the sea – The geologic story of south Florida*. Coral Gables, FL: University of Miami Press.

Holmes, C. W., R. Miller. 2004. Atmospherically transported elements and deposition in the Southeastern United States: local or transoceanic? *Applied Geochemistry* 19: 1189-1200.

IGS. 2006. Aquifer Definitions – Some useful definitions for talking intelligently about aquifers. Idaho Geological Survey. http://www.idahogeology.org/ (accessed February 24, 2006).

Kruse, S. E., J. C. Schneider, D. J. Campagna, J. A. Inman, T. D. Hickey. 2000. Ground penetrating radar imagine of cap rock, caliche and carbonate strata. *Journal of Applied Geophysics* 43: 239-249.

Loftus, W. F., M. C. Bruno, K. J. Cunningham, S. A. Perry, J. C. Trexler. 2001. The Ecological Role of the Karst Wetlands of Southern Florida in Relation to System Restoration. U.S. Geological Survey, *Water Resources Investigations* WRI 01-4011.

McNeill, D. F., K. J. Cunningham, L. A. Guertin, L. A. Melim, E. R. Warzeski, F. S. Anselmetti, R. N. Ginsburg, G. P. Eberli, P. K. Swart. 1996. *Data Report: Tertiary-Quaternary cores from the Florida Keys and Everglades*. South Miami, Florida: Miami Geological Society.

McPherson, B. F., C. Y. Hendrix, H. Klein, H. M. Tyus. 1976. The Environment of South Florida, A summary Report. U.S. Geological Survey, *Professional Paper* 1011.

NOAA. 2006. *Outreach – South Florida Ecosystem Education Project*. U.S. Department of Commerce, National Oceanic and Atmospheric Administration http://www.commerce.gov/ http://www.aoml.noaa.gov/sfp/outreach.shtml (accessed February 28, 2006).

Pollastro, R. M., C. J. Schenk, R. R. Charpenter. 2000. Undiscovered Oil and Gas in the Big Cypress National Preserve—A Total Petroleum System Assessment of the South Florida Basin, Florida. *U.S. Geological Survey, Open File Report*: 00-317.

Prager, E., R. Halley. 1997. *Florida Bay Bottom Types*. U.S. Geological Survey, Open File Report 97-256.

Scott, T. M. 2001. *Geologic Formations of Florida*. Florida Geological Survey digital file, 1:126,720. http://www.dep.state.fl.us/geology/gisdatamaps/state_geo_map.htm (accessed February 26, 2006).

SFWMD. 2002. *The Living Everglades*. The South Florida Water Management District. http://glades.sfwmd.gov/empact/home/index.shtml (accessed March 3, 2006).

Shinn, E. A., B. H. Lidz, R. B. Halley. 1997. IGC Field Guide T176: A Field Guide: Reefs of Florida and the Dry Tortugas. In *Geological Environments of Florida Bay and the Florida Keys Reef Tract*, comp. Tihansky, A., Prager, E., and Shinn, G.

Steinen, R. P., E. A. Shinn, R. B. Halley. 1995. Hypothesized fault origin for the rock reefs of South Florida. *Abstracts with Programs – Geological Society of America* 27 (6): 229.

Thomas, W. A., T. M. Chowns, D. L. Daniels, T. L. Neatherly, L. Glover, R. J. Gleason. 1989. The subsurface Appalachians beneath the Atlantic and Gulf coastal plains. In *The Geology of North America* F-2, Geological Society of America.

Warzeski, E. R., K. J. Cunningham, R. N. Ginsburg, J. B. Anderson, Z. D. Ding. 1996. Neogene Mixed Siliciclastic and Carbonate Foundation for the Quaternary Carbonate Shelf, Florida Keys. *Journal of Sedimentary Research* 66: 788-800.

Appendix A: Geologic Map Graphic

The following page is a preview or snapshot of the geologic map for Everglades National Park. For a poster-size PDF of this map or for digital geologic map data, please see the included CD or visit the Geologic Resource Evaluation publications Web page (http://www.nature.nps.gov/geology/inventory/gre_publications.cfm).

Appendix B: Scoping Summary

The following excerpts are from the GRE scoping summary for Everglades National Park. The scoping meeting was on January 24–25, 2005; therefore, the contact information and Web addresses referred to in this appendix may be outdated. Please contact the Geologic Resources Division for current information. For the full scoping summary, please visit the GRE publications Website (http://www.nature.nps.gov/geology/inventory/gre_publications.cfm).

Executive Summary

A Geologic Resources Evaluation scoping meeting took place in Homestead, Florida on January 24, 2005. The meeting was followed by a field trip on January 25, 2005. The scoping meeting participants identified the following list of geologic resource management issues. These topics are discussed in detail below.

1. The Florida Bay mud banks elevation and stability
2. Mangrove zone topography and buttonwood ridge height
3. Whitewater Bay and Gulf Coast estuaries
4. Solution holes
5. Aquifer characteristics and groundwater flow dynamics
6. Recreation and other use demands
7. Earthen and failed dams, canals, and sheet piling
8. Sediment transport and resuspension at Lake Ingraham
9. Sinkholes and karst features
10. Paleoclimates
11. Sea level rise
12. Geologic changes due to storms and hurricanes
13. Atmospheric deposition of African dust
14. "Lake Belt" management
15. Tree islands and hardwood hammocks
16. Archaeological sites

Introduction

The National Park Service held a Geologic Resource Evaluation scoping meeting for Everglades National Park at the Krome Center in Homestead, Florida on Monday, January 24, 2005, followed by a field trip the next day. The purpose of the meeting was to discuss the status of geologic mapping in the park, the associated bibliography, and the geologic issues in the park.

The products to be derived from the scoping meeting are: (1) Digitized geologic maps covering the park; (2) An updated and verified bibliography; (3) Scoping summary (this report); and (4) A Geologic Resource Evaluation Report which brings together all of these products.

Everglades National Park was established under Harry S. Truman's administration on December 6, 1947. On October 26, 1976, the park was designated as an International Biosphere Reserve. The park attained its Wilderness Designation on November 10, 1978. It was made a world heritage site on October 24, 1979, and was named a Wetland of International Importance on June 4, 1987. Everglades covers 1,508,537 acres spanning the southern tip of the Florida peninsula and most of Florida Bay between the peninsula and the Florida Keys. The Everglades is the only subtropical preserve in North America. The environments at the park vary from mangrove and cypress swamps, marine and estuarine environments, pinelands and hardwood hammocks, sawgrass prairies and rock ridges. The area includes a large portion of the Florida Bay, a large carbonate mud bank. The park contains some of the most pristine and unique marshland habitat in the continental United States.

Everglades National Park identified 385 quadrangles of interest. The Florida State Geologic Survey (FGS) has digitized a geologic map covering the state from individual county maps at a small scale (~ 1: 126,720 or larger). This map only displays 4 separate geologic units (Holocene sediments, Key Largo Limestone, Miami Limestone, Tamiami Formation) for inside the boundaries of the park. Located within the quadrangles of interest are 11 additional geologic map units.

Other geologic maps covering portions of the park itself include the FGS MS6/22 (1:24,000, 2000), the benthic habitat map published by NOAA CSC (1:48,000, 1999), Geological Society of America (GSA) Memoir 147 (1:79,000, 1977), the FGS OFMS 83/01-07 (1:100,000, 1996), 83/08-12 (1:100,000, 1995), 67 (1:26,720, Dade County), 66/01 (1:26,720, Monroe County), 63 and Series 120 (1:26,720, Collier County), USGS OF 97-526 (1:120,000, 1997) and 86-4126 (1:136,000, 1986). BEM Systems produced a hydrostratigraphy study for Big Cypress National Preserve and a small portion of the Everglades National Park that shows interpolated depth to the tops and bottoms of aquifer and aquitard layers. Additional mapping at a smaller scale will be more helpful for park management.

Significant Geologic Resource Management Issues at Everglades National Park

The Florida Bay mud banks elevation and stability

The Florida Bay is covered by an extensive system of supra- and subtidal carbonate mud banks, coastal marl ridges, coastal carbonate mud ridges, mangrove peat deposits, and mollusk deposits. There is a strong resource management need to understand how water moves around the bay and what buttressing effect, if any, the mud and marl ridges have on the flow of water. Another concern is gaining an understanding of the nature of landscape evolution during late Holocene sea level rise (23 cm [9 in] rise in sea level in 70 years). Many of the freshwater marshes behind the ridges are changing to super saline marine lagoons. The features in the bay are strongly related to minute changes in elevation. Environments can change within centimeters of topographic relief. Given the coverage of mapping at the park, normal surficial maps are not sufficient for complex management decisions at the Everglades. An interdisciplinary approach to mapping is critical to producing a useful product for resource management. Anthropogenic, supratidal, intertidal, subtidal, and coastal features would all be helpful. This holistic ecosystem approach integrates biological, physical, cultural, and oceanographic parameters. Lidar surveys in addition to satellite imagery, multibeam mapping, bathymetry data, water quality and circulation, shoreline change data, pre- and post-storm comparisons, oceanographic data (waves, tides, currents, turbidity, temperature salinity, sediment transport patterns, coral larvae and other species distributions), etc. are essential for resource management at Everglades National Park.

Research and monitoring questions and suggestions include:

- What is the relationship between coastal marl and carbonate mud ridges and the buttonwood distribution?
- What is the minimum mapping unit relevant to resource management?
- What are the flow dynamics (especially related to salinity) in the bay?
- What controls the distribution of the mud banks?
- Is there any remediation possible for the hypersaline environment in the central portion of the bay?
- Why does the basin and bank character of the Florida Bay resemble hexagonal mudcracks?

Mangrove zone topography and buttonwood ridge height

Mangroves thrive in oscillating fresh-saline water conditions. In a sense, they define the water level. A baseline needs to be established regarding sea level rise to determine its effect on the mangrove areas. Detailed topography would help manage this resource. The scale of inches is important for the low banks and ridges where the tides and wind expose the entire western basins.

Whitewater Bay and Gulf Coast estuaries

Whitewater Bay sits behind Cape Sable and is fed by the Shark, Broad, and Harney Rivers. It is bound by a buttonwood embankment growing as a natural berm on a storm beach made of mud.

Research and monitoring questions and suggestions include:

- What is the relationship between the diversion of water through canals and the buttonwood distribution?
- What is the nature of the Shark Slough-Taylor Slough divide?

Solution holes

Solution holes are an element of the karst topography at the park. They provide essential habitat for fish and other wildlife during the dry winter months at the Everglades. Solution holes occur throughout the park (especially in the eastern half) and need to be systematically located, mapped, and described for resource management.

Research and monitoring questions and suggestions include:

- How are solution holes and other karst features affecting water quality at the Everglades?
- Are solution holes sources of phosphorus input?
- How do solution holes affect the hydrogeologic regime including retention time, hydraulic head, and water storage?
- What is the relationship between water quality and karst topography?

Aquifer characteristics and groundwater flow dynamics

The interaction between groundwater flow and the overall fresh water and marine ecological quality must be quantitatively determined at the Everglades. Visitor uses and surrounding development are increasing the levels of certain substances in the water at the park. Nutrients from waste are causing algal blooms. Salinity levels are dependent on seasonal freshwater input and tidal circulation in the Florida Bay.

Research and monitoring questions and suggestions include:

- How many wells are necessary to model the hydrogeologic system at the park?
- Model the porosity and permeability of the Fort Thompson Formation.
- Examine the salt wedge characteristics versus the surface water.
- Is increasing the hydraulic head at the Everglades a good idea?
- How would an increase in hydraulic head from either concentrated precipitation or anthropogenic interference affect the local spring activity?

Recreation and other use demands

In 2004, Everglades National Park hosted 1,374,789 visitors, placing increasing demands on the limited resources and fragile ecosystem of the park. Motorized boat access and fishing are restricted in the wilderness areas of the park.

Research and monitoring questions and suggestions include:

- Are visitors affecting sediment transport and the hydrologic system at the park?

Earthen and failed dams, canals, and sheet piling

Dams and other earth works in the park pose a serious threat to the safety of visitors and park resources. During the 1930's, a series of canals and levees were constructed (including East Cape canal, Homestead canal, Slegel's ditch, Houseman's ditch, and Middle Cape canal) to divert the water away from the "prime" real estate around Cape Sable. The real estate venture failed and the land was later included in the park boundaries. The remediation of the canals and earth works is a park responsibility. Canals throughout south Florida divert water away from the natural flow between Lake Okeechobee and the Everglades. Locally, near Cape Sable and Lake Ingraham, the flow is disrupted and sediment transport patterns have changed. Fresh water marshes behind the cape are being salinated due to the overall lack of fresh water input.

Sediment transport and resuspension at Cape Sable and Lake Ingraham

The very nature of the landscape at the Everglades is one of change. Shifting muds and sands continually alter the shape and profile of the shoreline. Sand and mud erode from one beach and are deposited elsewhere in the course of a single storm event. A focus needs to be placed on understanding the sediment transport dynamics at the park. The hydrogeologic system in the area around Lake Ingraham was altered with the construction of canals, roads, and levees. As a result, sediments scouring through the canals are being deposited in the lake basin (6–30 cm/year, 2.4–11.8 in/year) and the lake levels are very low and bottom sediments are often exposed at low tide. The delta emanating from the Middle Cape Canal is expanding and increasing the sediment influx for the Florida Bay. Salinity is increasing as 80 high tides a year are cresting the low marl ridges. Higher salinity waters are encroaching on the fresh water areas. This leads to a decline in marsh, mangrove, and prairie areas.

Research and monitoring questions and suggestions:

- Are declines in mangrove, marsh, and prairie areas due to the canal system or due to sea level rise around Lake Ingraham or both?

- USGS survey points are too far apart for proper monitoring of landscape response to sea level rise (~400 m [1,312 ft] apart). Can the number of these points be increased?

- Should fill dams be destroyed or reestablished?

- What remediation can be done on the eroded canal openings (erosion rate is 0.6–1.2 m/year [2–4 ft/year])?

- What is the rate of change in sediment transport around Cape Sable?

- How much sediment is being lost through canal scouring?

- What would be the effects of replugging the Middle Cape Canal?

Sinkholes and karst features

The Fort Thompson limestone is a very permeable unit. Borrow pits and canals intersect this unit in many locations of the park. This is affecting water flow. Approximately 50 sinkholes have been located in the park. These serve as vital habitat during the dry season. However, their distribution, characteristics, depths, and interconnectedness need to be systematically mapped and described.

Research and monitoring questions and suggestions:

- What steps should be taken to model water flow in the park regarding karst features?

- Could aerial photography be used to map sinkholes?

- What is the relationship, if any, between solution holes and other karst features and the distribution of hardwood hammacks and tree islands at the park?

Paleoclimates

Cores in Florida and Biscayne Bays, and numerous sloughs in the park show peat and pollen as indicators of past climates. The spatial coverage for the cores is not at an adequate resolution to determine the temporal relationships and to make accurate interpolations between points. Bioturbation and other ground disturbances (railroad infill effects) distort the subsurface features.

Research and monitoring questions and suggestions include:

- Perform more coring operations to increase coverage at the park.

- Identify pollen species and correlate with paleoclimate.

Sea level rise

Sea level rise is affecting all of South Florida. While slowing the rate of sea level rise is beyond the resources of the park, monitoring sea level change and evaluating and predicting impacts on the park's landscape is a valid management issue. The fresh water marshes and brackish estuaries are under constant threat of inundation by the sea. Given the low relief of the park, this rise will destroy much of the marsh landscape protected at the park. Sea level rise is also causing beach erosion near Cape Sable and Lake Ingraham. Increases in turbidity with rising seas are causing large seagrass dieoffs and increased carbonate material suspension.

Research and monitoring questions and suggestions include:

- Is there any way to save the subaerial habitat from rising seas?

- What is the local rate of sea level rise?

- Looking at the affects of storm surges, how will the buttonwood and mangrove zones respond to the rising water?

- What direction should future planning proceed in light of the current restoration effort?

- Monitor and measure the relationship between water level flux and elevations to determine an exposure/submergence index (i.e. 100% of the time exposed versus 0% of the time exposed).

- Quantitatively define the terms subtidal, intertidal, and supratidal to use for future predictions and relate these to the local elevations and annual regime of water fluctuations.

Geologic changes due to storms and hurricanes

Storm events and hurricanes have a pronounced and often catastrophic effect on the landscape of south Florida. Baseline conditions must be determined and studied for the resource management to predict the environmental response. Hurricane Donna in 1960 evacuated water from the bay by about 1 m (3 ft), then the water rushed back in to a depth of 2.1 m (7 ft). This resulted in mud deposition on the south side of the mud ridges and a high-energy shell layer deposit on the north side. Hurricane Andrew blew the highland beach area near the Ross River away. Geochemical changes resulting from the influx of storm water went unmeasured during cleanup and restoration operations by local agencies.

Research and monitoring questions and suggestions include:

- Develop a response protocol in cooperation with other local agencies to determine the geochemical effects of storm surges.

- What are the recovery rates of mangroves after large storm events?

- Establish baselines for comparison and prediction of future events.

Atmospheric deposition of African dust

Dust has been blowing across the Atlantic Ocean and depositing in south Florida for thousands of years. Paleosols and reddish (oxidized) layers atop the Miami Limestone attest to these airborne inputs. The process continues today, but modern development has introduced nutrients, elements, microbes, pesticides, soot, organics, bacteria, viruses, and other contaminants to the dust. The dust diminishes air and water visibility. A peak of dust fall in the 1980s coincided with a sea urchin disease and other benthic die-offs. Lead, arsenic, phosphate, copper, iron, and mercury concentrations in the surface sediments in the middle of Florida Bay are highest in low tidal flux areas.

Research and monitoring questions and suggestions include:

- There are 9.1 m (30 ft) monitoring wells in the bay; these could be expanded and utilized (contact Gene Shinn).

- Did the combination of dust and hypersalinity kill sea grass and cause algal blooms in Florida Bay?

- Monitor dust levels and attempt to correlate with environmental responses. Are dieoffs caused by African dust or by the transport of sediments, nutrients, and organics transported out during rising seas and storms?

"Lake Belt" management

The term "Lake Belt" refers to a series of quarries near the park. These features are supposed to supply water to the park as part of a restoration effort. There is some concern about how these features are affecting groundwater movement. Some USGS monitoring wells are located near levees, but more wells would increase the understanding of the local hydrogeologic system. Local agriculture introduces sulphates, phosphorus, and other contaminants into the groundwater near these lakes that, given the permeable, conduit-rich bedrock, would easily contaminate the water in the quarries and affect the ecosystem of the park.

Tree islands and hardwood hammocks

Tree islands and hardwood hammocks are prevalent features at the Everglades. They dot the sawgrass prairies throughout the park. They appear to be oriented in linear trends. There is discussion as to whether the islands and hammocks are located in bedrock highs or lows. They could be located in peat depressions, or perhaps on a laminated duracrust formed by phosphorus from evaporites pulled up by the trees in the groundwater. Rock ridges, such as that at Rock Reef Pass, are subtle, enigmatic linear features on the landscape at the Everglades. There are approximately 20 rock ridges in south Florida. The amount of relief associated with these ridges is small, approximately 0.9–1.5 m (3–5 ft), but the vegetation changes across them and makes them appear more pronounced. Many theories abound as to why these features exist. Are they paleoshores, results of Pleistocene wrench faulting, developed fractures, concentrations of shells in oolite, paleo mudbanks, or the result of differential compaction and fracturing?

Research and monitoring questions and suggestions include:

- Can hydrogeochemistry determine if the bedrock is a source of phosphorous for these trees?

- How did the tree islands and hardwood hammocks form?

- What is the geologic control on their distribution?

- Are their linear trends related to elongated paleoflows?

- Obtain more cores in a transect through a rock ridge to help determine why they exist.

- Core tree islands to bedrock to determine the nature of their formation.

- Install a monitoring well into the tree islands to look at differences in local groundwater chemistry.

Archaeological sites

There are several sites, approximately 12,000 years old, along ancient coastlines that contain artifacts from the local indigenous populations. Mapping and/or reconstructing these sites would add to the cultural value of the park and help reconstruct the paleoshoreline in the 10,000 lakes, and Cape Sable areas especially.

Scoping meeting participants

NAME	AFFILIATION	PHONE	EMAIL
Andrea Atkinson	NPS, SFCN	305-224-4245	andrea_atkinson@nps.gov
Sonny Bass	NPS, EVER	305-242-7833	sonny_bass@nps.gov
Sid Covington	NPS, Geologic Resources Division	(303) 969-2154	sid_covington@nps.gov
Kevin Cunningham	USGS		
Robert Ginsburg	University of Miami, RSMAS	305-421-4875	rginsburg@rsmas.miami.edu
Melanie Harris	USGS, CCWS	727-803-8747 x3023	mharris@usgs.gov
Fred Herling	NPS, EVER/DRTO	305-242-7704	fred_herling@nps.gov
Todd Hickey	USGS	727-803-8747 x3040	tdhickey@usgs.gov
Kelly Jackson	University of Miami, RSMAS	305-421-4811 x4	kjackson@rsmas.miami.edu
Bob Johnson	NPS, EVER/DRTO	305-224-4240	robert_johnson@nps.gov
Harley Means	Florida Geological Survey	850-488-9380	guy.means@dep.state.fl.us
Sherry Mitchell-Bruker	NPS, EVER	305-224-4286	sherry_mitchell@nps.gov
Doug Morrison	NPS, EVER/DRTO	305-852-0324 x0327	douglas_morrison@nps.gov
Lisa Norby	NPS, Geologic Resources Division	303-969-2318	lisa_norby@nps.gov
Matt Patterson	NPS, SFCN	305-224-4211	matt_patterson@nps.gov
Anne Poole	NPS, Geologic Resources Division	303-987-6954	anne_poole@nps.gov
Tom Schmidt	NPS, EVER	305-224-4269	tom_schmidt@nps.gov
Eugene Shinn	USGS	727-803-8747 x3030	eshinn@usgs.gov
Dewitt Smith	NPS, EVER	305-242-7818	dewitt_smith@nps.gov
Trista Thornberry-Ehrlich	Colorado State University	757-222-7639	tthorn@cnr.colostate.edu
Brigitte Vlaswinkel	University of Miami, RSMAS	305-421-4918	bvlaswinkel@rsmas.miami.edu
Harold Wanless	University of Miami, Geological Sci.	305-284-4253	hwanless@miami.edu
Britton Wilson	NPS, SFCN		britton_wilson@nps.gov
Linda York	NPS, SERO	404-562-3133 x537	linda_york@nps.gov

Everglades National Park
Geologic Resource Evaluation Report

Natural Resource Report NPS/NRPC/GRD/NRR—2008/047
NPS D-345, September 2008

National Park Service
Director • Mary A. Bomar

Natural Resource Stewardship and Science
Associate Director • Bert Frost

Natural Resource Program Center
The Natural Resource Program Center (NRPC) is the core of the NPS Natural Resource Stewardship and Science Directorate. The Center Director is located in Fort Collins, with staff located principally in Lakewood and Fort Collins, Colorado and in Washington, D.C. The NRPC has five divisions: Air Resources Division, Biological Resource Management Division, Environmental Quality Division, Geologic Resources Division, and Water Resources Division. NRPC also includes three offices: The Office of Education and Outreach, the Office of Inventory, Monitoring and Evaluation, and the Office of Natural Resource Information Systems. In addition, Natural Resource Web Management and Partnership Coordination are cross-cutting disciplines under the Center Director. The multidisciplinary staff of NRPC is dedicated to resolving park resource management challenges originating in and outside units of the national park system.

Geologic Resources Division
Chief • Dave Steensen
Planning Evaluation and Permits Branch Chief • Carol McCoy

Credits
Author • Trista Thornberry-Ehrlich
Review • Linda York and Carol McCoy
Editing • Melanie Ransmeier
Digital Map Production • Stephanie O'Meara and Trista Thornberry-Ehrlich
Map Layout Design • Melanie Ransmeier

The Department of the Interior protects and manages the nation's natural resources and cultural heritage; provides scientific and other information about those resources; and honors its special responsibilities to American Indians, Alaska Natives, and affiliated Island Communities.